Praise

"Cindy Halvorson's love of people overflows in this gentle and inviting volume. She teaches preachers not just how to read biblical texts better, but how to read people in those texts. Using context and characterization details, she shows how to make movies with words, so the biblical people come alive. More important and unusual on this topic, she focuses on their faith. She ministers Christ to them in the details of their needs and, in so doing, ministers joy and hope to readers."
—Paul Scott Wilson, emeritus professor of homiletics, Emmanuel College, University of Toronto, Toronto, Canada

"Having heard Cindy Halvorson preach about the wine steward's amazement when Jesus turned water into wine (John 2:1–12), I was eager to learn from her. *Real People, Real Faith* delivers. Cindy understands the power of story over facts. She offers a pathway into the biblical narrative that gives the preacher a unique style, one that invites the listener to encounter God in a personal way."
—Becky Balestri, pastoral leadership revitalization program manager, Omaha Presbyterian Seminary Foundation

"Preaching is not simply a cognitive or academic experience. Those who hear a sermon have meaningful questions, real needs, and deep joys and sorrows. Cindy Halvorson helps us understand that to preach to the whole person, we need to preach the whole story. Context, personality, and spirit all matter. Her book gives insights into a wholistic way to connect God's story to our story and share a word of hope, love, and grace."
—Todd Buegler, senior pastor, Trinity Lutheran Church, Owatonna, Minnesota

REAL PEOPLE,
REAL FAITH

REAL PEOPLE,
REAL FAITH

*Preaching Biblical
Characters*

CINDY HALVORSON

Fortress Press
Minneapolis

REAL PEOPLE, REAL FAITH
Preaching Biblical Characters

Cover Design: Emily Harris Designs / Tory Herman / Kristin Miller

Print ISBN: 978-1-5064-6966-9
eBook ISBN: 978-1-5064-6967-6

To all the faithful preachers,

when you are energetic and when you are not,

when you are faith filled and when you are not,

when you are strong and when you are not,

when you are confident of your call and when you are not,

may you encounter the Divine and know
you are deeply loved, highly valued, and always enough.

CONTENTS

PREFACE

When I agreed to write this book, the world was not reeling from a pandemic, nor were we under stay-at-home orders. Racial protests were happening in other communities, and my heart was heavy for the situations, but they weren't taking place in my backyard. Politics were . . . well, politics, or at least what politics had become at this time of history when everyone seemed divided. And then a whirlwind of events began changing the world—the globe, the nation, and my husband's and my personal world. Both his parents and mine struggled—with strokes, cancer, and surgery, and one stepped from this world into the next.

I often wondered what to preach when I had the opportunity to be in the pulpit. I needed encouragement and hope. I assumed others did too. I needed help to extend grace and forgiveness to those who arrogantly confronted me. I assumed others did too. I needed peace and perseverance to make it through the day. I assumed others did too. I found what I needed in the pages of Scripture. The Divine graciously met me in the passages I read, studied, and pondered. Preparing my sermons became a solace. My mental, emotional, and spiritual well-being was fortified as I experienced the power of the Living Word.

PREFACE

Through the years, I have developed the storytelling preaching style I propose in this book. Working on my doctorate, which focused on this preaching style, caused my thoughts and ideas to shape, coalesce, and mature. This style may or may not be a good fit for you as a preacher. We each preach in ways that complement who we are as people, and we each grow and morph as our experiences influence us. As I look over the past twenty years, my life's journey, and my connection to Scripture and the Divine, I realize that I have changed significantly. The engagement with Scripture I discuss in this book has enriched my connection to the Ever-Present One. Others tell me this manner of relating to the Holy Narrative has enriched their lives as well. I pray that twenty years from now, when I look back again, I will see continued growth and a persistent connection to God. May we all allow Scripture, the Living Word, to change us.

I want to extend words of appreciation: To Fortress Press and Working Preacher, you asked if I would consider writing this book. I only dreamed about the possibility, but your invitation made the way for it to become a reality. You gave courage to this preacher. To Beth Gaede, my editor, you guided, provided suggestions to, and encouraged me in this journey. You are a gift! To the congregation at First Baptist Church, Owatonna, Minnesota, you extended immense grace to me as I practiced and developed my preaching style. You granted me time and support while I pursued my doctorate, participating in feedback groups, surveys, and interviews. I thank God for you! To my family and friends who have encouraged me, prayed for me, and believed in me, you are my village! To my husband, Greg, you're still the one. And to the Divine, the Giver of Grace upon Grace, the Lover of my Soul, you have my eternal gratitude.

1

Preaching for Mind and Heart

As preachers, our relationship with Scripture can be . . . complicated. We interact with these sacred texts—reading, studying, listening, and pondering—all the while wondering how to communicate a meaningful word for those who listen to our preaching. Some of us are enchanted with the process and outcome of wrestling with Scripture. We find the turning and re-turning of the phrases and words to be joyful parts of our call. And yet there are times we discover—or at least suspect—we have little, or nothing, to say that hasn't already been said about a particular text. We might even find the passage to be perplexing, unclear, or somewhat frustrating.

nothing to say

As preachers, we seldom confess these challenging experiences. To add to the difficulty, we are aware—or at least I hope we are—that we engage in a type of foolhardiness. How can we, as imperfect humans, speak with any level of confidence to the concepts in these sacred and holy texts? How can we translate the truths, the thoughts communicated two thousand years ago, in a pertinent and meaningful manner that can be easily comprehended and applied in our current world? We carry a passion in our souls, longing to impact those who listen to our words, our wonderings, our assertions. We pray that those listening come to the preaching event with the expectation to be challenged or encouraged or motivated or somehow moved in their spirit. The weight, the gravity, the sheer responsibility of communicating such holy precepts can cause even the most gifted preachers to tremble. We shy away from discussing this dynamic interplay of delight and distress, joy and frustration, the thrill and trepidation we encounter as we grapple with the responsibility of preaching. Yes, many of us have a deep, soul-satisfying experience when we interact with Scripture. And yet numerous preachers also stoop under the weight of preaching Sunday after Sunday. We hold dear the sacredness of these texts, and because we highly value Scripture, we impose great expectations upon ourselves (and others too) concerning the "right" way of comprehending and communicating it.

Putting One Foot in Front of the Other

The subject of preaching and engaging with Scripture holds personal importance for many of us. I'm convinced that the ways in which God is understood or described impact people's ability to encounter the Divine. Years ago, I mentioned to a small group that had gathered to study Scripture that we are all theologians, each having an understanding of God. The men and women around the table looked at each other quizzically and with disbelief etched on their foreheads. Yet when I began to ask them questions about God, they had answers. Whether their answers

Thoughts about God = theology

arose from teachings they encountered as children or what they heard TV preachers say, they had thoughts about God.

Those concepts impacted how they approached the Almighty. Would God be forgiving? Was the Divine calculating a person's goodness? How far away was this Keeper of the Heavens? Did trivial details matter to the Creator? Was the Holy One of Scripture still active in people's lives today? All of these thoughts impacted how each person at the table would engage with the Lover of their Souls—that is, if it is even acceptable to mention God. I was no different. The way God had been described to me and the understandings I had as a child intertwined to create my personal comprehension of this Infinite Being.

I grew up in a church that highly valued knowledge of the Bible. I sat through thousands of sermons, Sunday school lessons, and other experiences of listening to a Scripture reading followed by some form of teaching. As children and teens, we participated in games and competitions focused on our knowledge of the Bible. We were expected to do personal devotional readings daily. This approach afforded me a solid grounding in the knowledge of the Scriptures, and I am thankful for that foundation. However, for me, this didactic approach, while rich in information, remained dry and lifeless. This experience of retaining biblical knowledge, while feeding my desire to excel, affirmed my personal sense of being flawed. If knowing the Bible gave a person value, I interpreted my inability to know it *all* as proof that I had fallen short. Being fixated on knowing information from Scripture, I was unable to translate the intellectual information into a vibrant relationship with God. I knew facts and data but was stunted in my emotional, relational, and spiritual growth as a person and as a Christian.

Didactic approach — dry & lifeless

When I was nearing thirty years of age, I heard a preacher comment in passing that the Gospel of Mark makes mention of Jesus's emotions. This was not the preacher's point; it was merely a tangential statement. However, it caught my attention. Invigorated by that piece of information, I decided to read through Mark's Gospel with the intention of noticing the emotions of Jesus. Having been raised in a Euro-American culture with a strong Scandinavian influence, I viewed Jesus as a stoic individual, likely to be without emotion. I assumed that if he had feelings, he kept them well controlled . . . except for that one time with the money changers in the temple. Besides, I had heard countless sermons on the need to control our feelings. The espoused thought was that emotions could not be trusted. Following one's feelings would lead to foolish behavior at best and evil reactions at worst. The intellect, reason, and logic were highly superior to any emotion a person might experience. However, as I read Mark with this deliberate attention to emotion, I was amazed. Right there on the pages of Scripture, I observed a Jesus I hadn't known existed. The Markan Jesus seemed human and touchable, someone with emotions and experiences and with whom I could connect. This experience changed my practice of reading and engaging with the sacred texts of the Christian tradition. I saw Scripture differently. The Bible was no longer pages filled with data and information for me to memorize. Instead, it became a living text revealing the Divine to me in a way I had not known before. My hunger for interacting with Scripture became insatiable.

Suddenly, Jesus and the other characters of the Bible stories I thought I knew so well seemed different. They were more real, more lifelike and less plastic, less artificial. They had personality traits I had never considered. I reasoned that if the characters in the Bible were more authentic than I had understood, it was probable their difficulties in life were more genuine as well. This line of thinking caused me to wonder, Was their faith more alive than I had comprehended? And if their faith was more dynamic than I had previously understood, had I also misunderstood who their God was? This wondering was an invitation for me to enter into a relationship with the God and characters of Scripture I had previously not experienced. The way I engaged the sacred texts was changed.

Years later, after having gained a seminary education, I was asked to speak at a women's retreat. The retreat was held off-site, away from the revered sanctuary of the church. I took the different setting as permission to be more creative with my comments than I was when I occasionally preached on a Sunday morn- *jmash* — ing. Since I had always loved stories, I surmised it might be a workable opportunity to retell a story from the Gospels. Armed with my imagination and the knowledge I possessed concerning Israel in the first century CE, I crafted a message for the retreat. As I wrote the sermon, my heart was warmed more than usual. The depth of emotional connection to the biblical characters and their plight surprised me. However, the greater experience was my sense of connectedness to the Divine Love displayed in the story. I was eager, and a bit timid, to share my carefully enhanced story with the women at the retreat. They would be expecting a more traditional approach to the Scriptures. I worried about how they would receive it but pressed on with my creatively developed story.

Following the message, the women's comments confirmed that their hearts, too, had been touched. Some stated they had never understood that particular story the way I told it. Others expressed sentiments that confirmed my own experience of connectedness to the Loving Healer revealed in the account. This type of imaginative storytelling as a way to engage with the sacred texts appeared to be meaningful . . . at least in a retreat setting.

Years passed before I again considered trying this imaginative storytelling approach to creating a sermon. The catalyst for doing so was my experience with my congregation. I stood in the pulpit looking out at the dear souls sitting in the pews staring back at me. I had been pastoring this church for a few years, and I had preached through the lectionary cycle and wondered what else I could say that might be meaningful. The congregation included people of such a wide range of ages and experiences. Some had been in church for decades, teaching Sunday school for young and old; others were younger adults and newer to church. The older, more experienced group caused me some concern when I thought about preaching. What could I say to them that they didn't already know? And for the younger adults and families, how could I preach the Scriptures in a way that might impact their experiences and interactions with God?

I wanted the congregation members to connect with the Divine in a way that enriched their lives. Most of them didn't need more biblical information or exploring of the original language within the text. Their hearts weren't craving another self-improvement sermon or a step-by-step homily to evoke new habits. They needed what the characters of Scripture needed: to meet and engage with the Giver of Life. Could I craft a sermon that would create space for them to encounter the Holy One? Would I dare to move away from an intellectual exchange of thoughts and concepts and try to communicate to both mind and heart? Was it possible to retell a biblical story in such a way as to make room for people to engage with God? And did I have

intellectual ↳ heart

enough courage to preach an unusual sermon, in an unusual style, on a usual Sunday morning?

In the years that followed, I began telling stories from the Bible. The congregation was filled with grace as I carefully experimented with breathing life into the characters of Scripture. When I began this homiletical adventure, I didn't fully anticipate where the journey would lead. However, I began to yearn to develop a methodology for crafting these enhanced Bible stories. The desire to continue growing intellectually and spiritually while being more intentional about reaching the heart of the listener resulted in the pursuit of a doctorate in biblical preaching. Engaging in the educational opportunity offered by Luther Seminary required reading and researching what others had to say about preaching, as well as conducting and analyzing original research. Finally, I had an excuse to ask the congregation members the questions I had been longing to ask. Surveys and interviews became part of congregational life. Those who participated presented information, kindly worded criticism, and helpful suggestions that I would not have heard otherwise. I am grateful for their offerings. *THESIS*

What I learned in my research and methodology for bringing biblical characters to life through preaching is the subject of this book. Through the years, my preaching style has morphed. I suspect this is true for all preachers. What I offer in this book may be meaningful to you. It may not. My prayer is that you encounter the Divine.

Why Do We Preach?

And so I go back to the beginning. Why do we preach? The preacher who preaches almost every Sunday needs a good reason to continue wrestling with the Scriptures and attempting to communicate its truths in a meaningful way. Yes, preaching is a significant tradition within our Christian heritage. Some would even say it is foundational to the life of the church. The apostle Paul claimed that the proclamation of the gospel message is necessary for people to hear the good news of the One in whom they can believe (Rom 10:14–15). Communicating the truths of Scripture through preaching is the dominant feature of worship services in many Christian churches.

A couple of years ago, a group of students sat around tables in the seminary's preaching lab. They would each write and deliver several sermons to their classmates throughout the semester. Some were beginners, not having had the opportunity to preach in a church or campus setting. Others had preached several times, whether on a Sunday morning or to a group of campers or as part of campus ministry. As their instructor, I posed the question, "What do you hope to accomplish with your sermons?" In other words, what is your purpose in preaching? Why do we preach? I gave them a few minutes to jot down their answers before they would share them with the group. As they shared, a recurring theme presented itself. At that point in their journey, most of them concluded that preaching was a way of sharing information with the audience. Of course, they were right. But were there other reasons to preach? One of the students, who had been doodling on the piece of paper in front of her, spoke without looking up: "I preach in order to encourage people." I smiled. That student gave a reason to preach that didn't emphasize the mind. She was the only one.

The focus on the intellect saturates our Western way of knowing and understanding our world; consequently, preaching has been aimed at the intellect, the mind. The desire to affect the

8

listener's thinking is scriptural. Romans 12:2 instructs the reader to "be transformed by the renewing of your mind." The author of Philippians gives the directive to "think about such things," the things that are "true," "noble," "right," "pure," "lovely," "admirable," "excellent," or "praiseworthy" (4:4–8). Colossians 3:2 states clearly, "Set your minds on things above." Preaching to the intellect can be meaningful. Cognitive psychologists would agree, since a person's thinking often shapes their lives. Many of us can attest to the fact that having new information presented to us at a critical point caused us to make an important change or reach a different conclusion than we had previously held. The Enlightenment bolstered the importance of rational thinking and scientific discovery and called into question suppositions that could not be proven with data gathering and logical formulations. Our current culture highly values cognitive ability and training. Facts and logic are esteemed, while intuition and hunches are suspect.

However, humans are more than a brain or mind. We possess mind and heart, intellect and sentiment, thoughts and feelings. In a time when scientific data and measurable outcomes seem to drive society, many people are craving an artistic, relational, and right-brained approach for engaging with the Holy. Consequently, preaching that aims only at the intellect, the rational mind, the left brain, presents a problem for the hearer in that it only addresses one component of our humanness. Having listened to sermons for years, I wonder if the goal of many preachers, both past and present, is to create an intellectual assent to the concepts of Scripture, believing the "right" things in the "right" way while living in a "right" manner.

Unfortunately, numerous lifelong churchgoers have shared with me that intellectual assent alone left them spiritually stunted. These dear souls affirmed my own experience of intellectually knowing the "right" information but remaining far from the Redeemer. Their love of God and neighbor had not increased. Their trust in the benevolence of the Divine had not grown. Their generosity in love, forgiveness, and grace refused to blossom. While ideas, information, and instruction have their place, sermons must not be limited to these. When proclaiming the Word, if God is presented only as a concept, a barrier may well be formed, limiting a person's ability to know the Lover of our Souls relationally.

The good news is that we do not need to be bound by such limitations. Understanding Scripture as a compilation of stories and teachings that invite the reader/listener into a vibrant relationship with the I AM empowers individuals toward spiritual vitality. James 4:8 invites the audience to "come near to God." But how can a person come near to God if the Holy One is only a cerebral concept? Keeping sermons locked in the mind hinders many from relationally encountering the Redeemer. Listeners remain stranded in their attempt to develop a relationship with the Giver of all good gifts when the Divine is only represented as a theory or proposition to be intellectually mastered.

While many preachers have different goals for their sermons, the goal I return to again and again is to create space for the listener to encounter the Divine and thus experience the life-changing work of the Holy Spirit. This is the fundamental story of characters in the Bible. Yes, their intellect was involved, *and* it was their encounter with the Almighty, the Lover of their Souls, that was life-changing. Mary Magdalene exclaimed, "I have seen the Lord!" (John 20:18), and the disciples joined her refrain: "We have seen the Lord!" (John 20:25). The encounter with the Lord made the difference.

Henri Nouwen writes, "Hospitality is not to change people, but to offer them space where change can take place."[1] Knowing God as a hospitable God, I have concluded that the goal of sermons is to accomplish the task of hospitality. Hospitable sermons intentionally create emotional and intellectual space for the listener to connect with the Healer. Consequently, the preacher must move beyond presenting Scripture as merely ideas, information, and instruction.

Considering the Reader

While the task of sharing biblical concepts often rests upon us as preachers, according to Karl Barth, an influential theological mind of the twentieth century, it is important to recognize that preaching the Word of God "does not take place in a vacuum. It has a human counterpart . . . [for a] specific people . . . in a specific place at a specific time."[2] Barth's acknowledgment of the listener reminds the preacher that effective preaching must give thought to the audience.

Listeners differ, adding to the challenge of communicating the truths of Scripture in a meaningful way. Hearers' exposure to and understanding of the Bible vary. Particular congregation members are steeped in Scripture, having read it and some having taught it for years. Yet some of the most astute listeners find themselves wondering how to connect biblical concepts to their daily lives. Other individuals have had little contact with biblical stories and concepts. Some wonder if scriptural claims are true. Reaching all groups in a valuable and life-impacting way can seem impossible. The complexity of effectively communicating the Word compels those who preach to search for ways to bridge the gap between Scripture and listener.

When we consider the listener, those of us who preach must contemplate various styles of communication. Today's listeners are not the same as those in the pew seventy-five years ago. Our exposure to and understanding of the global world have expanded radically in the past few decades. People travel internationally and interact with different cultures. Another significant change is that information is readily available. Ask Siri or Alexa or Google your question, and you are likely to have an answer immediately. Do an internet search, and you will have plenty of information to consider. This access to information and a variety of teaching/learning styles has caused education to morph. Teachers are no longer the only source of information. Educators consider whether a student is more visual or auditory, left-brained and logical or right-brained and creative, introverted or extroverted, plus so much more. Creative projects are assigned to reinforce the student's understanding of concepts. Group projects enhance the experience and learning for the student.

And of course, the way we communicate has undergone significant changes in our society within the last several decades. People years ago used a telephone that was attached to the wall to briefly communicate information. When a person answered the phone, no one asked where they were. It was obvious they were at home, standing close to the wall, talking into the phone. Now we chat with people while we drive (hands-free, of course). And many times, we communicate by typing a message into our handheld devices instead of talking. There's also the matter of how we are buried in advertisements. When we seek information, commercials crowd our screens, inviting us to watch a video about a product we don't care about so that we can repair a problem we didn't know existed. Social media has given everyone the opportunity to share the details of their lives, as well as their opinions, should they choose. The happenings of the international world are presented with live footage and emotional responses from those interviewed. Some people regularly interact with multiple mediums of communication and information at the same time. We adjust and change along with our society.

During the early days of the Covid-19 pandemic, when live sporting events were canceled, sports channels aired games from years gone by, referred to as "classic" sports. My husband and I sat down to watch a classic World Series game. We immediately noticed that the score wasn't displayed in the corner of the screen during the entire game. We had to wait for it to be shown. The batter's statistics were mentioned by the announcers, but there was no graphic, no chart, no spreadsheet to accompany this information. The bottom of the screen did not have a running update on other sporting events. Within two decades, the communication of sports information had thoroughly changed. I'm sure you could give many more examples.

With such significant changes occurring in our communication, our information gathering, and our teaching/learning experiences, it stands to reason that our preaching must change too. The preaching style of yesteryear no longer seems as effective as it once was. Lectures filled with data and information on Scripture, explanations about the nuances of a passage's original language, and additional biblical passages that support a text's claims appear to have lost their impact. As a society, we have changed how we consume information. In our typical day, when we are presented with statistics and ideas, we experience color, movement, and graphics. Our attention span for dry information has, well, dried up. While sermons spoken in a lecture style were sufficient in their day (some would argue that they were not truly "sufficient"), today's preacher needs to cultivate more creativity in order to reach the listener.

When I was interviewing some congregation members as a part of my original research for my doctoral thesis, I expected some of the younger people to express a desire for more engaging sermons than the lecture style of the past. But what surprised me were the comments of the older people—one octogenarian in particular. He sheepishly confessed that in the past, he had developed a habit of "not listening to the sermons" because they were "typically boring" and did not connect to his life.

As a society, the ways we receive information—whether through television, movies, or the internet, whether on big screens or handheld devices—have forever changed communication. As communicators of Scripture, we can no longer ignore the expectation that a sermon be delivered in a manner that captivates the current listener's attention. It is rare, or maybe even impossible, for a listener to engage with the substance of the sermon if their interest is not held. Barth summarizes the issue well: "Preachers must not be boring."[3]

The responsibility of reaching the listener in a meaningful way resides with the preacher and can seem daunting. No wonder we feel discouraged from time to time when we consider the task of preaching. Maybe you can identify with the ministers who have commiserated with me as we wonder how to best share theological truths. Our belief that Scripture can be meaningful, life changing, and heart transforming increases our desire to effectively communicate the Word to our specific congregations. How does the preacher stay true to the text while speaking in a compelling way to an audience who is detached from the passage by time, space, and culture? The original audiences who heard and read the Scriptures were not removed from the text by language or analogy. The agricultural references used by Jesus were a part of their everyday life. The earliest hearers understood the lifestyle within the stories. The mentions of political and religious power did not need explanation. The ways people lived their lives and performed religious duties were common for many. The original hearers of the Gospel writings could frequently relate to the characters in the biblical stories. After all, the stories were their stories. The concerns were their concerns. The desires were their desires.

The current reader or listener of Scripture experiences a distance of time, geography, worldview, and societal norms from the text. This separation often diminishes the multifaceted characters of Scripture into flat, one-dimensional, superficial figures with whom few can identify. Many theological scholars have treated the characters of Scripture as one-dimensional, as if they merely serve the purpose of the lesson within the story. If the biblical witnesses are left lifeless and one-dimensional, how can their encounters with their God be meaningful to an audience so far removed by time, space, and culture? The God of Scripture may also appear hollow and fictitious, which is certainly not the intent of the authors. Could preachers better reach listeners by breathing life into these witnesses within Scripture? Could the God of these characters become more than a distant figure from above?

Scripture tells the stories of characters who experienced fears, needs, and desires, and they encountered the Divine, causing their lives to be changed. The biblical witnesses possessed behavioral traits and personalities, and God met them at their point of need. These encounters were life altering for many within the pages of our holy text. Allowing the characters of Scripture to come to life within our sermons is a helpful tool to utilize when our preaching is aimed beyond the intellect to include the heart.

Throughout this book, I will share ideas for creating sermons with a focus on breathing life into biblical characters, allowing them to possess archetypal fears and other emotional struggles. While the biblical world remains distant from today's society, the human emotions experienced by the persons of Scripture remain the same. My experience is that when biblical characters are portrayed in a sermon in a way that acknowledges human emotion and struggle, the listener is better able to identify with the characters in Scripture. This enables the listener to hear with their heart, not only their mind. During the interviews that I conducted for the original research for my doctorate, many people shared with me that the ability to relate to the character and story enhanced their ability to connect with the Divine. I pray that you, too, will experience a deepening connection with the Lover of your Soul as we engage with the concept of moving preaching beyond intellectual assent of ideas, information, and instruction toward an ongoing, life-giving connection with the I AM. I suspect that as I write, I, too, will have a deepening experience. Praise be to God!

Breathing life into biblical characters —

2

Honoring the Stories

When I was growing up, my siblings and I would ask my parents to tell us about their childhood. "Tell us a story about when you were little," we would say. For years they obliged. My dad told and retold the story of throwing rotten eggs at the side of the chicken coop. The smell didn't deter him and his brother from the activity. He also shared that when they ran out of rotten eggs, they began pitching good eggs at the building. Apparently, my grandparents disapproved of my dad's and uncle's behavior. We would giggle at the thought of my dad behaving in such a mischievous manner. We had only known him as a hardworking, no-nonsense adult.

My mother told and retold the story of using a bedsheet as a parachute. She and her brother each grabbed two of the four corners of the cotton cloth and leaped off the roof of their two-story house. The bedsheet hadn't worked the way they planned. Every time she told us of their escapade, we gasped. Our mother? She was cautious and concerned about safety . . . especially ours.

Our experience of our mother included phrases like "Be careful" and "Don't get hurt." There was more to this woman than met the eye . . . at least the child view that we possessed. Years later as I recalled her tale, I wondered if the parachute experience enhanced her need to remind us to be careful.

My husband's relatives were, and continue to be, fantastic storytellers. Whenever there was a family gathering, the uncles would sit around and tell story after story of the generation before them. We cringed and shuddered every time we heard the story of the hitchhiker who kept sticking his hand inside his jacket, causing the uncle to wonder if the vagrant had a gun. Other times, our cheeks ached from laughter as we heard of the relative who got his foot stuck behind his head and had to "roll home" to get help.

Stories of my grandfather's work ethic, forward thinking, and innovative reasoning have encouraged us to work hard and courageously reach beyond the present. My husband's family has spent hours telling tales of their great patriarch and matriarch. Their mission work in Madagascar, which included building a school and educating others, is legendary and inspirational, impacting their children, their grandchildren, and generations to come.

Those in my generation also recounted anecdotes with our children about our childhoods—trying to ride a bike with closed eyes to experience what it might be like to be blind, rubbing together the noses of two neighborhood cats, or feeling certain that an alligator lived under the bed. The tradition of storytelling continues as our children now tell tales to their children. The stories connect us and give insights into the generations before us. They teach us, entertain us, and sometimes inspire us.

Stories bring us closer together. Humans are influenced by the stories they hear and tell. Throughout history, people have communicated through stories. From the time of drawings on cave walls; to ink, quill, and parchment; to the word processor, tales have communicated truths, fables have taught lessons, and sagas have transferred values from one generation to the next. Until the last few centuries, societies had been largely illiterate. Only scholars could read and write. Sharing stories allowed people to espouse and learn the values of their community. Still today, we enjoy and learn from a well-crafted story. We blink away tears as we watch a movie with a story that connects with our own emotional experience. We laugh at sitcoms as we follow the story line week after week. Many of us sense a connection with the characters in the stories, whether on the big screen, on the small screen, on the stage, or around the dining room table. Stories are powerful. Connection to the past, a sense of identity and belonging, values of the culture, and so much more have been, and continue to be, communicated through stories.

Scripture is filled with stories. Let me restate that: Scripture is *the* story, the story of God, the story of the Divine lovingly inviting humanity into relationship, the story of the benevolent Life Sustainer who cared, and continues to care, for all human beings. The earliest passages of the Bible are stories of a people telling anecdotes to connect all generations with the God they worshipped, the Rescuer who had cared for them and provided for them. The Gospel writers followed this pattern, communicating their experiences with Jesus, as well as his teachings. This engagement with stories linked past generations and future generations with the God of *the* story.

I am grateful for science and technology. My life is significantly improved due to these innovations. However, through the years, some people have come to think of these mechanisms as the only way to influence or teach, creating doubt in the value of stories. Discounting the influence of a good story has impacted the ways we preach. Many have replaced powerful stories with concepts and calls for behavioral change. Scripture presents excellent examples of verbal communication used to teach—to challenge concepts and modify behaviors. The prophets of old confronted false claims about Jehovah and challenged iniquitous and unjust behavior. Jesus taught the multitudes designs for godly living in his Sermon on the Mount/Plain, as well as in other settings. He also chastised the leaders of his day for fraudulent behavior. Paul, John, Peter, and others who wrote letters to the churches of the first century CE admonished the churches to whom they wrote to adopt correct theology and honorable behavior. Yes, the preacher must impart concepts and beliefs, moral standards and ethical practices, theology and discipleship.

And . . . The word *and* is important to me. It reminds me that there's more, expanding my perspective. Let me show you what I mean by using the word *and* in a compound sentence. It is the preacher's responsibility to teach theology and encourage discipleship, *and* I observe people moving toward the Giver of Life through story, especially through anecdotes that create space for the listener to encounter the Holy. Our sacred texts are filled with stories. We read tales of God inviting people to walk with the Divine (Abraham; see Genesis). We hear biblical narrations of the Rescuer liberating people from oppression (children of Israel; see Exodus). Surprising sagas describe the Almighty partnering with people against all odds to defeat evil (David and Goliath; see 1 Samuel 17). I could list many more, but I'm confident you get the picture.

When the prophets of old were making a point, they told of their visions and utilized stories and images to which people could relate. Nathan rebuked King David concerning his sin against Bathsheba and her husband, Uriah, by telling a tale about a poor man with only one ewe lamb (2 Sam 12). Isaiah spoke of a burning coal on his lips (Isa 6:6–7). Ezekiel relayed an epic account about dry bones having life breathed into them (Ezek 37). Jesus used fables to connect with his audience. Whether spinning a tale of someone hosting a grand banquet and all the invited guests choosing to do something other than attend the event (Luke 14:16–24) or laying out an account of a rich man and a beggar named Lazarus (each having an after-death experience; Luke 16:19–31) or telling the saga of the one who searches for lost treasures—a sheep, a coin, or a son (Luke 15)—Jesus masterfully wove together stories to convey spiritual truths. The writers of the Gospels recounted anecdotes of people who had encountered Jesus, including children who were blessed (Matt 19:13–15), thousands who were fed (Mark 6:35–44), lepers who were healed (Luke 17:11–19), a blind man who was given his sight (John 9), and more. Throughout the Gospels, people were transformed when they encountered the Ever-Present Love through Jesus, whether in person or through story.

Midrash

We can see that stories were used in significant ways throughout Scripture, from the earliest pages of Israel's history to the prophets and in Jesus's teachings. The Hebrew tradition treasured its sacred texts. When the people were faithful, they memorized them, wrestled with them, tied strips with the printed words on their hands and foreheads, wrote them on their doorposts, and based their lifestyle upon them. The Law of the Lord was theirs, even while it was God's story. God and they, together, partnered to create the narrative. Their history, God's story. God's story, their history.

Since much of the Jewish tradition and interpretation of the sacred writings were temple-centered, the destruction of the temple created a significant challenge for the rabbis of the first and second centuries CE and beyond. Midrash was one of the techniques the ancient rabbis used to interact with their revered texts. They noticed nuances within the passages and wondered about them. What was the purpose of using an uncommon word? Why were there "apparent contradictions, omissions, or duplications within the narrative arc"?[1] While holding the Scriptures in high regard, the rabbis spurred each other toward creative thinking as they contemplated these nuances. Finding a conclusive explanation was not the goal; creating an opportunity to contemplate the Holy was.[2] This interpretive method acknowledged that holy manuscripts held more meaning, more wisdom, than what was expressed in the exact verbiage written on the scroll. Multiple meanings could coexist, each understanding touching the heart of a variety of listeners/readers. Freedom and space existed within the text for deeper knowing. Reflecting on the text and asking questions of what was absent in the writing provided methods for wrestling with the sacred account. It was believed that what was missing from the narrative was as important as what was present. The absence of details in the recounting of the saga was an invitation to wonder and question and maybe find one's self in the story. Following the rabbis' tradition of midrash, preachers of the Christian faith have grappled with the Holy Scriptures using their biblical imagination. The Spirit of God invites us to find our place within the sacred text, and the stories in the Gospels allow us to wonder about the meaning within a passage.

These explorations will certainly feed our souls and enrich our preaching.

We, as preachers, are compelled to communicate the truths of the Living Word in a relatable, meaningful way. Using our imaginations and wondering about the details that are *not* shared enhance the possibility of uncovering a deeper meaning from the text, one that unites with our hearts, our fears, and our hopes. Tenets of the Christian faith claim that God meets us in our fear and hope, sorrow and joy, mind and heart. Consequently, we must learn to translate the stories of the Scriptures into stories that can relate to our listeners' lives, stories that address the archetypal experiences and emotions that we understand as the core of being human.

Thank You for Asking

While we bring our hearts and minds, our passions and curiosity, to Scripture and allow them to break open the text for us, we do so in a spirit of deep humility. I was one of the presenters at an annual workshop about preaching. During one of the breakout sessions, I stood in front of the group of twenty-five preachers. Armed with a marker and a flip chart, I was discussing the very topic of this book: preaching biblical characters. I touted reasons for breathing life into the characters of Scripture and using a biblical imagination in the process. As I began to lead the participants through an exercise in order to engage in the process, one preacher raised his hand. I enthusiastically called on him, grateful for his involvement. He was concerned: concerned that I might not be respecting Scripture, concerned that I was encouraging a methodology that would lead people astray, concerned that I was on a slippery slope toward profaning the holy texts by adding to Scripture. Immediately I wished the workshop was two hours long instead of only one. I wanted to spend an hour discussing how we, as preachers, approach Scripture; where the authority of the Christian canon resides; and how we understand the text. Instead, I smiled with a gleam in my eye and said a heartfelt "Thank you for asking." At the time, he didn't realize that his devotion to the Holy Narrative aligned with mine. Because of time constraints, I replied with a paragraph or two and asked him to stick with me through the process before passing any judgments. But oh how I wanted to wade deeper into the discussion of reverence for the Holy Scriptures.

When approaching Scripture, it is imperative that we come in humility, bowing in heart and mind to the Spirit and the text. Our souls must be open. This is one reason it is crucial to pray, to quiet ourselves in the presence of the Teacher, assuming a listening posture before and during our encounter with any passage. Our arrogance can get in our way, hindering our ears and our hearts from receiving the message the text has for us. While it is vital to prepare our hearts to receive the text, I am grateful the Spirit can hurdle the barriers we bring—all the mixed-up motives, the noise of our lives, and the distractions along the way.

Years ago, a few of my colleagues and I met together for spiritual renewal. This was a planned quarterly event. As was our custom, one person chose a passage for our time together. The plan was for us to prayerfully listen to the reading of the text, quietly waiting for an inspiring or encouraging word that would minister to our hearts. Our fellow pastor announced the reference, and I smirked. Weeks earlier, I had turned that exact passage over and over in my mind, studying it for hours as I prepared for speaking at a conference. The entire experience, from studying to writing to delivering the message, had been rewarding. Certainly, I thought, I had squeezed out every drop of meaning from the passage my colleague was preparing to read. I approached the experience doubtful that I would gain anything more from the text. I listened to the reading and then sat quietly with the group. The experience was profoundly humbling. The Spirit of God reached beyond my arrogance and ministered to my soul anyway. It was a lesson to remember.

Whenever we interact with the sacred text, it is crucial that we acknowledge that our particular experiences create a lens through which we comprehend everything, Scripture included. We bring with us our personalities, our upbringings, our experiences, our education, our cultures, our worldviews, and so much more. Every aspect of our being impacts the way we understand Scripture. It can be difficult to identify our personal lens as we encounter the text, but an awareness that we have a lens, a viewpoint, a perspective that impacts our understanding is a good starting place. Hopefully, the acknowledgment that we have a perception will lead us to ask, "How might this passage be read by another person, someone with an experience other than mine or someone of a different culture or gender or socioeconomic status?"

The authors of Luke and Matthew display a great example of the need to understand the holy texts from another's perspective. The Lukan account of Jesus's teaching about the poor states, "Blessed are you who are poor, for yours is the kingdom of God" (Luke 6:20). Yet Matthew shifts and adds a different layer to the meaning of Jesus's sermon: "Blessed are the poor in spirit, for theirs is the kingdom of heaven" (Matt 5:3). If the hearer is living in a subsistent mode day to day, concerned about feeding their family, the Luke version might hold greater meaning. If the hearer is financially comfortable, Matthew's words deliver a weighty challenge to the heart of the listener.

Honoring Scripture requires us to acknowledge that these sacred texts were written for others—not just to those who understand the world as we do. For that matter, the Holy Narrative was written for them . . . not us. While believing that we, too, are included in the text, we must acknowledge that the original authors of Scripture didn't have us in mind when they put ink to papyrus. Experiencing the Holy Spirit working in these same texts in our lives evokes, we can hope, a true humility within our hearts. Understanding the world from our own perspective is natural and unavoidable. Yet as we mature in our connection with the Divine and the Holy Narrative, we are obliged to also recognize that Scripture is written for all.

Confidence in our knowledge must be held lightly, since our comprehension is limited and quite possibly flawed. When we interact with Scripture, the subject is God. Scripture informs us that God is beyond our understanding. As God responds to Job's cries, the Almighty lists question after question to communicate the finite nature of human beings in comparison to the incomprehensible Great Mystery (Job 38–41). The author of Isaiah 55 poetically declares that the Lord says, "For my thoughts are not your thoughts, neither are your ways my ways. . . . As the heavens are higher than the earth, so are my ways higher than your ways and my thoughts than your thoughts" (vv. 8–9). As we grapple with Scripture, humility toward God and the text is mandatory. Openness in our spirit must prevail.

Being True to Scripture

Being true to our sacred texts is essential. When I have talked about allowing a biblical imagination to invigorate our connection to Scripture, some listeners have expressed apprehension about going beyond what the text explicitly states. I appreciate their concern, *and* we have biblical examples of people interacting with Scripture beyond what is plainly stated and understood. Jesus in the Sermon on the Mount repeatedly says, "You have heard that it was said. . . . But I tell you . . ." (Matt 5:21–22, 27–28, 33–34, 38–39, 43–44; see also vv. 31–32). The author of Luke, in relaying the experience on the Emmaus road, writes, "And beginning with Moses and all the Prophets, he [Jesus] explained to them what was said in all the Scriptures concerning himself" (Luke 24:27). As Jesus expounded on the Scriptures, it is safe to say that the explanation went beyond what had previously been understood. The explanation and amplification of the holy texts are the terrifying tasks of preachers and teachers. Thoughtful and faithful expositors of Scripture desire for their words to be "pleasing in your sight, Lord, my Rock and my Redeemer" (Ps 19:14).

Being true to the sacred texts requires us to be shaped by the Word, not for us to shape the Word. Being true to the biblical canon compels us to not make claims about the Divine that are false or in error. Being true to the Holy Narrative means staying true to the purpose of the stories of Scripture—to invite people into the ongoing story of God. Our desire to be true to Scripture goes beyond the consideration of what we *do* with the words and concepts. It must also include what we *do* with style. The sacred texts were and are filled with a liveliness that we dare not present as dry and lifeless. The powerful stories and characters within the pages of the Bible, the narratives and their witnesses, must be portrayed as much more than flat, one-dimensional cartoon sketches. The characters within the sacred stories experienced the Ever-Reaching One reaching for them. They, in turn, embraced a relationship with God. Just as Jesus desired for his disciples of the first century CE to have a vibrant relationship with the Light of the World, so Christ yearns for intimacy with God's people today.

Reading, Studying, and Percolating

Coming to the sacred texts with humility implies that we intend to engage with the Scriptures. This Living Word has been entrusted to us. We must be good stewards of the precious and powerful Scriptures.

My editor, Beth, to whom I am beholden, asks great questions: *Why is this important? Is there a stronger word to use to communicate the depth of this concept? What is the difference between these two words?* These questions, and many more, helped me articulate what was rolling around in my thoughts. While writing about the preacher's engagement with Scripture, I wrote the phrase "whether reading or in-depth study." Beth asked for clarity. What had seemed like a simple phrase suddenly begged for an explanation.

Reading: Scripture was originally read aloud, possibly to an individual, but more likely to a group of people. Today, the Bible has been printed and translated and is readily available to much of our world. Due to the increased literacy of our day, some individuals are encouraged to adopt a daily habit of personal reading. This can be a meaningful spiritual discipline. There are aids to guide and inspire people as they read through the Bible in one year, or maybe three years, by following a calendar with an assigned reading for each day.

In-depth study: Taking time to dig into a passage can be rewarding. The sacred texts were written in a language other than my native tongue. This is likely true for you too. Even if your native tongue is Hebrew, Greek, or Aramaic, language morphs over time. Looking at the study aids for the original language can help the reader have a deeper understanding. Comparing various translations and wondering about the word choices of the translators can reveal a truth that might be otherwise missed. Reading commentaries—current, older, and much older—can deepen the richness of the passage.

Percolating: "Percolating" wasn't a part of the phrase about which my editor asked, and yet it is a significant piece of our encounter with Scripture. This word is not original to me; one of my seminary professors would encourage us as students to let a passage "percolate" within us. I like the word. It is the practice of letting Scripture roll around in our minds and hearts while we mow the yard or chop vegetables, go for a walk or paint the bedroom. "Percolate" gives me permission to muse and reread a text, wondering why a phrase sticks out for me or sticks in my craw. This takes time and space of mind and heart. Creating space of mind and heart is a process requiring focused wanderings and wonderings.

What we expect from Scripture impacts our approach to interacting with the text. I wonder how our lives would be changed if we were to anticipate and listen for the Divine as we engaged the Word. Often, we come to the text looking for teaching or instruction. When our hearts and minds are open, the Spirit can remind us, challenge us, and comfort us.

The Power of Scripture

Our belief concerning the power of Scripture to transform hearts and lives influences how and what we preach. The Bible, the blessed compilation of sixty-six books composed by numerous authors across the span of hundreds of years, informs us of God's intentions for humanity. It is a beautiful masterpiece of human authorship guided by the Spirit. At the time of writing, the human and Divine partnered together. And at the time of reading or studying or preaching, the human and Divine partner together again. This partnership is a holy endeavor. And while a partnership exists, we defer to Scripture. We bend to the text; the text does not bend to us. Our desire is to be formed by the narrative; the narrative is not to be formed by us. As we bend to and are formed by the Word, we recognize the beautiful power that transforms us.

Authors of old knew this power too. The psalmists who penned Psalms 19 and 119 were convinced the Word of God, the Law of God, the Commands of God, had the power to impact lives. They dedicated nearly two hundred verses within those two psalms to communicate this truth. The author of Isaiah 55 confidently reported the Lord declared, the "word that goes out from my mouth . . . will not return to me empty" (v. 11). The writer of Hebrews, agreeing with the words of the psalmists and prophets, reiterated these truths to their Christian audience, saying, "For the word of God is alive and active. Sharper than any double-edged sword, it penetrates even to dividing soul and spirit, joints and marrow" (Heb 4:12). The power of the Word changes our lives, our hearts, and our minds.

Understanding Scripture

Preaching is directly impacted by the ways we as preachers understand and wrestle with the sacred texts. This likely seems obvious. Yet sometimes, the obvious needs to be examined. Without considering the ways we comprehend Scripture, we might find ourselves approaching it by examining only what we think is available within a passage itself.

Looking at the Holy Narrative through a literal lens is a starting point for those who long to understand the Bible. Literalism connects with the human developmental stage that longs for certainty. Our desire to know the formula so we can control the outcome begs us to be literalists. If I do *this*, then *that* will happen. Acknowledging that a passage (or even Scripture as a whole) may have multiple meanings makes us uneasy. The literalist in us tries to lessen our uneasiness by grasping for the most obvious, everyday understanding. When there isn't an obvious understanding, we begin to craft principles that the passage might uncover.

The symbolic and allegorical modes of comprehending add depth to a text. For example, the rich symbolism used to describe the Holy aids our understanding. Psalm 23 claims the Lord as shepherd. Jesus picked up this figurative language in John 10, saying he is the good shepherd. Then he stretched the symbol of shepherd to also claim that he is the gate for the sheep, enhancing listeners' and readers' understanding of Jesus as shepherd. The Gospel of John is saturated with symbolic and allegorical language that Jesus used to explain who he was. Jesus didn't limit himself to shepherd language. He also used other symbolic titles, such as the Living Water, the Bread of Life, the Light of the World, the Resurrection and the Life, the Way, the Truth, and the Vine. Christians have capitalized on this imagery for millennia to aid their understanding of the I AM. When we explore figurative speech, symbolism, and allegories, we see that there is more to understanding Scripture than the literal, take-it-at-face-value methodology. As we turn the literary devices over and over in our minds and hearts, we uncover meaning that we had not previously known.

When we wrestle with a certain text, we can turn to other passages to assist in informing the passage. The author of the Gospel of Matthew makes several references to the Hebrew Scriptures in order to inform the content of Matthew, beginning in chapter 1. Jesus instructed his disciples by utilizing various passages from Moses and the prophets (Luke 24:27). Comparing one Epistle to another is a worthy exercise in our attempts to comprehend the meaning. Allowing the songs of the Hebrew Scriptures to enlighten the connection to the early church deepens our understanding of the whole. All of Scripture is connected. It creates its own context. We must not claim that a group of verses communicates something that would not fit into the overarching theme of the Holy Narrative.

Remember, the canon is a compilation of writings. While other biblical passages might aid and form our understanding of a text, we also need to look at each book within our Scriptures as a piece of literature. The writings are related, *and* they are distinct. Each book has a unique theme. The various books have particular forms and styles for communicating their specific messages. The Gospels are a great example of distinction. Each Gospel writer portrays Christ in a certain way to a specific audience, communicating to that group precise teachings and stories for their explicit need. Keeping in mind the connectedness and the particularities of a text while wrestling with the passage can yield fruit that can be missed if we are not mindful of these concepts.

As theologians and preachers, it is essential that we ruminate (or percolate) on a passage. As the text rolls around in our minds, our hearts have the opportunity to connect to the passage in a way other than simply intellectual. Different phrases stand out to us. We find nourishment for our souls, and our lives are enriched. Our ability to persevere is strengthened, and the Divine leaves an imprint on our hearts. As we look at the text from various angles, we wonder and we consider. We ponder and we question. Asking questions of a passage frees us to discover aspects of the Divine that we had not known.

Recently I preached from the assigned Gospel reading of the Revised Common Lectionary: Matthew 13:1–9, 18–23. Jesus speaks to the crowd and discusses the four soil types and the way seeds grow in each variety. In the later verses of the assigned text, Jesus explains the meaning of the parable. Permitting the passage to roll around in my mind and heart, I began wondering, Why wasn't the sower careful when planting the seeds? Asking this question while pondering and wondering about the passage shaped my sermon. (I wish we were face-to-face so we could have a discussion. I would love to hear your thoughts.)

Looking in the cracks, peering through the peepholes, stepping into the dimly lit room of a text, and letting our eyes adjust promise to reveal deep meaning, maybe even veiled meaning, that has always been there but we had not recognized. By intentionally peering into a text, the passage seems to be granted permission to grow and morph, reaching deep into our lives. We, as students of a text, are invited to transform along with the passage.

Sitting in one of the theology classes required in seminary, I was introduced to the model of the Wesleyan Quadrilateral.

Although John Wesley did not craft and articulate the concept as we know it today, he used the underlying methodology in his learning and interactions with sacred texts. He has been credited with intertwining four sources for theological reflection. The four considerations are Scripture, tradition, reason, and experience:

* Scripture: What does the Bible say? Is the concept found in more than one place within the Scriptures?
* Tradition: How have the Mothers and Fathers of our faith understood it? What has the church embraced in years gone by? What do the faith traditions, creeds, and dogmas say about the concept?
* Reason: How do discerning thoughts enlighten the perspective? What are the scientific discoveries that inform our knowing?
* Experience: What is the human experience? What is your personal experience?

Different denominations place a greater value on one of the four than on the others. Some advocate for *sola Scriptura*, "Scripture alone." Others understand Scripture from the perspective of their denominational traditions. Appreciating logic and scientific discoveries cause some to marvel at the vastness of the Divine. Valuing personal experience leads some to read the text through their personal lenses. Because I believe the Ever-Reaching One surpasses our attempts to understand, I have no need to wade into the debate. Suffice it to say that all have value; however, the combination of the four creates a strong filter to use when interacting with the holy texts. Having an interdisciplinary structure for interacting with Scripture will enhance our connection to the Living Word. Being guided by these four categories, we can wonder about scriptural concepts and engage in the midrashic tradition, pondering the details of a story that have not been scripted. Allowing our biblical imagination to wander empowers us, as preachers, to explore the texts for various meanings that may be deeper than what is immediately observable.

Through the years, I have observed the Holy Narrative being used as a guide to life or a how-to manual for right living or right thinking. The blessed canon is so much more than a recipe book or a script of formulas for thinking correctly or behaving righteously. Our sacred text is the Living Word of God. Life changes, resulting in our need for different priorities or new ways of understanding the Lover of our Souls. This Living Word is dynamic, partnering with the Spirit to teach, encourage, and shape us, also allowing us to encounter the Giver of all good gifts. Because the Word is the Living Word, it isn't enough to rely on last year's understanding, the last decade's conclusion, or the last century's suppositions.

When our children were in elementary and middle school, we bought a boat. It was ten years old when we purchased it. We were as giddy as children on Christmas morning to have this small "fish 'n ski" boat. The first summer that we owned this new-to-us toy, we went to the lake four or five times a week. I struggled a bit the first summer we became boat owners. My husband appreciated good cooking and gathering around the dining room table. This was the way we had dined most evenings for years. But now that we had a boat—at least during the first couple of years—every time I put together a large dinner to be eaten at the table, my husband and children were disappointed. After a couple of delicious but disappointing meals, the comment was made that the family would rather have sandwiches and go to the lake than have a delicious meal while staying home. Priorities had shifted. Adjustments to past expectations could allow for more enjoyment as a family.

Interacting with the Living Word requires that we approach Scripture without past expectations of meaning. Life's experiences change us. Priorities shift. Needs develop. The Living Word is just that: alive. It can handle the fluctuations of life. The Spirit, through the Living Word, meets us in times of consistency and predictability, but it also, perhaps especially, meets us in times of fluidity and change.

The Living Word

It is helpful to consider the way we comprehend Scripture. Do we hold it as rigid and antiquated, only teaching and guiding those in centuries gone by? A static document that aids our understanding of religious history? A formula empowering us toward our best lives? Or do we see it as living and active, able to touch our spirits today? The author of Hebrews declares that "the word of God is alive and active" (4:12). The writer of 1 Peter describes God's word as "living and enduring" (1:23). The sacred texts can be effective modes through which the Lover of our Souls speaks to us.

Holding my cup of coffee, I gazed out the large picture window in my dining room. Most mornings, I set aside some time to read my Bible and meditate while I savor the dark roast. That morning was no different, other than my schedule wasn't as full as usual, allowing me to be more relaxed in my routine.

I turned my eyes to the text in front of me and began reading about Moses's experience with the burning bush as told in Exodus 3. Somewhere between the verses, this passage was no longer about Moses. It became God's words to me: "I have . . .

seen the misery of my people. . . . I have heard them crying. . . . I am concerned about their suffering. . . . I have come down to rescue them. . . . I am sending you" (vv. 7–8, 10). The One who calls us was calling me. My spirit was humbled and happy, terrified and at peace, confused and content. My physical heart was pounding. My eyes were overflowing. My nose was dripping. I didn't know what the future held for me. I just knew that I had to say yes. In that moment, the Living Word was active and alive in my heart, speaking a specific message to me, . . . and my life changed due to that experience.

Not every experience with the Living Word is that dramatic or that significant for one's calling. Sometimes we hear simply a whisper that reminds us that God is present or that shifts our understanding of the Redeemer or widens our love for our neighbor or deepens our commitment to the ways of Love. We can be assured that the Holy Initiator will speak to all who have ears to hear. This includes clergy and laity, professional and volunteer, teacher and student.

Since power resides in the Living Word, we, as preachers, can take a deep breath and remember that our calling is only to present the Living Word. Yes, we have a responsibility to use our talents, skills, and time as necessary to give a faithful sermon; however, it is the Word that is powerful. I make this distinction to alleviate the stress that many preachers carry. We do not bring about change. The Living Word does that. We are not responsible for speaking to each circumstance. The Living Word does that. We cannot challenge all people, comfort all people, confront all people, console all people. The Living Word does that. It is our responsibility to present the Word, and that responsibility is not to be taken lightly.

Stories of Scripture

Mark Ellingsen, a Lutheran pastor and author, wrote, "We must tell the story instead of just using it as an example."[3] Too often, the story within a text is used to shape a concept that the preacher wants to impart to the listener. Yet being truly true to Scripture allows the story within the Holy Book to invite the reader/listener into God's story. In our desire to be true to Scripture and honor the Living Word, we are compelled to consider the lens we pick up as we approach a passage. As we read, study, and allow the sacred texts to percolate within our minds and hearts, we will experience the power of Scripture. Sometimes the experience will be riveting and life changing. Other times it will be a gentle whisper or an invitation into the silence. We desire for our congregations to be moved toward spiritual vitality and meaningful existence. Consequently, our hearts are energized, and maybe a bit terrified, when we think about sharing these rich texts with those who are willing to listen. The style of preaching that I am proposing in this book begins with the details of the text, then moves to the Spirit-led imagination of the preacher, creating space for the listener to become more open to the Divine. May we be emboldened to tell the sacred story.

3

Capturing the Contexts

My friend and I walked along the sidewalk of my neighborhood, talking in the ways dear friends with a long history have a tendency to chat. At one point, the conversation turned toward my research project for my doctorate. I said a few scholarly words about using one's imagination to impact one's preaching style in order to engage the listener, hoping that I sounded very intelligent. My friend grinned, because she knows me. My opportunity to impress her with my intelligence had evaporated years before. And still she listened, asking thoughtful questions.

Then she shared a recent experience. The youth minister at her church had preached the previous Sunday morning, telling an updated version of the story of Zacchaeus. In the sermon, the speaker referred to the character as "Zack," who came down from the tree and invited Jesus to his house for a "pizza party." The preacher gave the characters of the biblical story a speaking dialect befitting a California surfer, with phrases such as "Hey, Dude." My friend admitted that she had been perplexed. She appreciated the attempt to make the story relevant to today's culture, but at her core, she found it "distracting and distasteful." Replacing Zacchaeus's setting with "Zack's" context wasn't beneficial, at least not for her. Instead, it created difficulty for her as she tried to engage with the sermon.

Often when biblical characters are lifted out of their context, the listener instinctively struggles to relate to them. If the goal as a preacher is to be creative, then "Zack and a pizza party" accomplishes the task. But if the goal is to engage the listener, removing characters from their context can create a barrier for the person listening. Creativity can be entertaining and can cause the audience to continue listening. But we want more than just an entertained listener. We desire an engaged listener, one who ponders and grapples with implications of the narrative, one who experiences the power of the Living Word. Such engagement is the outcome of a partnership among the listener, the preacher, and the Spirit. This partnership creates an opportunity for the listener to experience the story—and more importantly, the God of the story.

The context of the story has implications for the story; it is the holding place for any narrative and helps generate meaning for the account. Apart from the context, the words can imply various meanings, some of which would be incorrect. When people hear about an event, they often ask when or where it happened, essential details if the story's meaning is to be clear. A simple statement such as "It snowed two inches overnight" needs context. Did that happen in January in Minnesota? If so, then it is to be expected. Or did it happen in January in Dallas? If so, the entire Metroplex is at a standstill. Or did the snowfall happen in May in Minnesota? If so, the speaker is likely to be exasperated. Even the greatest snow enthusiasts are weary of winter and eager for warmer temperatures in the month of May. Context matters.

The biblical stories didn't take place—nor were they told—in a nebulous vacuum. The context aids and shapes our understanding of the details that are highlighted in the narrative. We will unpack this more throughout this chapter. Assuredly, the incidents occurred in a certain place and time and involved a specific person or people group. The authors of the biblical books chose which details to include. The particulars shared by an author enhance the meaning of the passage in direct correlation to the context. The story of Nicodemus in John 3 is a good example. The author of John tells us Nicodemus's role and title. He was a Pharisee and a member of the Jewish ruling council. Readers familiar with the hierarchy of power in the context of first-century CE Israel understand that he was not an uneducated, common man struggling to understand Jesus's teachings. He was highly educated and widely respected. And still he was confused but intrigued by Jesus's teachings. This detail shapes the story. How was Nicodemus, an educated man accustomed to possessing knowledge, feeling, since he lacked understanding? The context and the specifics of Nicodemus's position deepen the reader's/listener's ability to relate to the story. These descriptions can move us beyond the intellectual understanding of God—and who we think God to be—to include the psychological discomfort when uncertainty overcomes our previous knowledge of the Divine. (By the way, uncertainty in our faith journey occurs in everyone's life as we continue growing spiritually.) Being true to Scripture includes paying attention to those aspects. Often, the details of the context are essential in grasping the full impact of the biblical narrative. But context is multifaceted.

Context of Scripture

The need to be true to Scripture has already been established. As we engage with the Holy Narrative, whether we are doing personal study or planning to preach, we need to attend to various contexts, the most crucial being the scriptural context. Often, it is helpful to contemplate the author's theme. Each book, or Gospel, has one or more premises that the author intends to illuminate. When wrestling with the Gospel of Luke, the wise preacher considers the recurring theme of Jesus including the marginalized in his ministry. This theme might impact our understanding of a parable or story. As the preacher allows a passage from John's Gospel to percolate within their heart and mind, considering Jesus's resounding "I AM" claims might impact what seems important in that text. Verses from the Acts of the Apostles are likely to be influenced by the author's attention to the workings of God's spirit.

Any story in Scripture is placed within the larger framework of the text, whether the Hebrew Scriptures or the stories within the Gospels. However, when we look particularly at the Gospels, we realize the events recorded for us in them are not in chronological order. This is a greater concern to those of us who live with a Western worldview, since we are well trained to think in a linear fashion. Other societies, both today and in the past, view stories as valuable tools for communicating meaning and values, not simply a means of transferring data to the listener. The authors of the Gospels made choices about the overarching story they told, placing certain anecdotes and teachings together and arranging their materials in sequences that in themselves have meaning. So we must ask why a certain story is placed where it is within the Gospel account. Why did the author of

Matthew include the story of feeding the five thousand immediately before the story of Jesus walking on the water and Peter
getting out of the boat? Is there a connection between these stories and Peter's declaring that Jesus is the Messiah two chapters
later? Or what is the meaning of the author of John telling the
stories of Jesus feeding the five thousand and then walking on
the water yet never mentioning Peter stepping out of the boat?
How does Jesus's claim that he is the Bread of Life connect to
the feeding story? The authors of our sacred texts chose which
stories to include, where to place them in the larger writing, and
which details to share.

Historical and Cultural Context

The historical and cultural context of a narrative also impacts its
meaning and our understanding. The worldview of the original
audience of a text will be different from our viewpoint, with its
Western influence. How did the first listeners understand the
value of people or animals or property? In what ways did these
cultural views impact males and females, elders and children,
property owners and tenants? Much of the biblical world was
influenced by a strong patriarchal and hierarchical order. How
did that impact the woman who "had been subject to bleeding for twelve years" (Matt 9:20)? Her encounter with Jesus was
undoubtedly affected by this order of power.

Economic conditions need to be considered as well. What
did it mean to be a day laborer in the first century CE? Who were
the wealthy people, and how did they gain their riches? Another
crucial detail that would impact every aspect of every story in
the Gospels but is infrequently mentioned is the fact that the
Jewish people lived under Roman rule. Their land was occupied

by the Roman government and military. What fears might the citizens of Jerusalem have lived with? How did inhabitants of Israel understand going along to get along? What were the differences among the Pharisees, the Sadducees, and the Essenes in their understanding of their faith tradition and their interaction (or lack thereof) with the politics of the day? Researching and learning about these various historical and cultural circumstances add deeper understanding to the Scriptures and set the stage for releasing the characters within these stories from their confines as flat, one-dimensional caricatures. Commentaries and reputable online sources can be helpful in gathering the information required.

Each preacher will have their own style for including the historical and cultural information. I assure you, listeners can make the journey into a different culture and time. They are well practiced at this exercise. Theatrical productions, movies, fictional and nonfictional stories, and even video games move their audience to another time and place. The listener expects to step into a different setting. Weaving the historical and societal details throughout the sermon, referring to these cultural assumptions, can be helpful to the listener as they journey into the biblical narrative with the preacher.

The Physical Environment

Geography, terrain, and climate might also add meaning to the sermon. I think of Jesus's use of the rocky soil in his parable of the sower (Matt 13). The importance of the terrain for the parable's meaning is quite evident.

Being mindful of the environment of the scriptural passage also helps the hearer relate to the story and connect with the character. The natural environment impacts us. We know what it is to walk up a hill and feel winded. At least, I assume I'm not the only one to have experienced this phenomenon. We have felt the surprising pain of stubbing our toes when the path is rocky. We've faced the heat of the midday sun and wished we could find some shade for relief. The characters of Scripture also knew these sensations. When the preacher refers to these conditions, the listener can begin to identify with the biblical characters.

The author of John's Gospel tells the story of the man born blind (John 9). Where was the man when Jesus saw him? According to John 8:59, Jesus was leaving the temple grounds. Did Jesus encounter the man inside Jerusalem on a road near the temple, or was he outside the city? What kind of experience would this man have had as he tried to walk to the Pool of Siloam? Did he follow a well-worn road? How did the arid climate impact his experience? All of these considerations enrich the story. Some of these details shape the story.

Time of Day, Time of Year

When the authors of Scripture indicate the time of an event, it is likely a factor to which we need to pay attention. It isn't necessary, or even wise sometimes, to make this detail the center of the sermon, but it can certainly add to our understanding of the text.

In Mark's recording of Jesus's early ministry, the author points out that Jesus prayed "very early in the morning, while it was still dark" (1:35). I have heard preachers use this verse as support for their claim that this is the best time of the day to pray. People were encouraged to set their alarms earlier than necessary for family and work routines to allow time to pray. I admire the commitment to prayer, and the early morning timing might certainly be beneficial for some, especially if their minds are fully engaged early in the morning. But for those of us who need our first moments of the day to be *after* sunrise, preferably with a cup of coffee to help remove the cobwebs that have developed in our brains overnight, well, there just might be a better time of day for purposeful prayer. For some, rising while it is still dark is likely to create an unintentional nap time instead of focused prayer time.

But what if we allow ourselves to wonder about the reference to the time of day instead of using it as a concept to shape our spiritual disciplines? What caused Jesus to get up so early? Was the mat where he slept uncomfortable, so he couldn't sleep well? Did he choose to pray during the moments when sleep eluded him? Was he so excited to participate in ministry that he couldn't sleep? Was his spirit so fully alive due to the prior day's experience of healing people and setting them free from evil that his brain was running and planning how to serve others in nearby villages? Considering the context of the time of day enriches the anecdote and allows various understandings.

The timing in the seasonal or yearly calendar, the religious calendar, or the weekly calendar impacts the story too. Is there a significant Jewish faith tradition connected to the timing? In what way is the day of the week or the festival timing significant to the meaning of the passage? Does the event happen on the Sabbath? Or is there urgency to complete a task because it is the day before the Sabbath?

Let's think again about the story of the man who was born blind. Jesus healed him on the Sabbath (John 9:14–16). The text tells us that this healing on the Sabbath was problematic.

However, let's wonder a bit further. What did it mean for the experience of the man who was born blind? How did the Sabbath impact the man's walk to the Pool of Siloam? The author of John also includes the time of year, the Festival of Tabernacles, but we have to go back to chapter 7 (vv. 2, 10, 14, 37) to find this information. (Remember the significance of context within the Gospel book. If we simply lift the story out of its context, we miss these details.) How does this timing impact the man? Jerusalem is likely to be bustling with people during the week of the festival. And yet it's also the Sabbath. Is the Pool of Siloam more crowded than usual? Who might be at the pool? What could the disciples be encountering during this incident?

The time of year also suggests details such as if it is planting, growing, or harvesting time and a rainy or dry season. Jesus repeatedly used the time of the year to enhance his parables. His listeners could connect with his teachings because they understood the rhythms of their lives. Again, commentaries and reliable online sources can inform us as we ponder the context of time within the sacred stories.

Enhancing the Point of the Story

As I have unpacked the various aspects to consider when contemplating the setting, I hope you have been able to delight in the richness of the texts we have inherited. Being true to Scripture demands that we consider the contexts. The added benefit of exploring contexts is the increased possibility for the listener to relate to the story. The goal for the retelling of biblical stories is to create space for today's listener to identify with the character and their needs, and then when the character encounters the Divine Love revealed through Jesus Christ, the listener will identify with the character and make that connection as well.

Authors, storytellers, and communicators make choices in how to convey the message they want the listener or reader to grasp. Any given passage of our sacred text allows the preacher to make choices as well. Yet for those of us who are concerned with staying true to the text, options are limited. We are not given a blank slate. The preacher's responsibility to honor the intentions of the original author (as best we can) and engage with the text for our contemporary audience informs our choices. While the preacher has creative liberty, the imaginative choices cannot contradict Scripture.

Let's consider the account of the woman at the well (John 4). The preacher has creative license when describing the details of her walk to the well. Does she walk on a rocky or smooth path? Is the neighborhood quiet, or do we hear restless animals in the distance? However, her walk cannot take place at night, under a starlit sky. The passage tells us otherwise. The climate of Samaria permits us to wonder whether there was a breeze as she walked to the well. However, the storyteller cannot claim that it's cold and snowy. The story must be congruent with Scripture.

The details we choose to include in a story can enhance the listener's ability to identify with the woman of John 4. The image of her walking a rocky path could be developed to articulate her struggle: "She walked along the path, staring at the rocky terrain. It seemed to be mocking her and all the rocky experiences—the hardships, one after another—that were her life." A slight breeze can add to her longing: "She noticed the slight breeze with gratitude. It provided relief from the heat of the sun. She couldn't help but wish for relief from the drudgery of her existence." Choices around the imaginative elements of the anecdote can be used to offer listeners an opportunity to relate to the character, but they must remain contextual in every sense.

Holding the various contextual details, we can begin crafting a sermon that is both imaginative and true to Scripture. The skillful preacher is able to share a great deal of information and data with the listener, yet the purpose of the sermon is to create space for the hearer to identify with the character and their needs so that the listener will also encounter the Redeemer.

Let's again consider Nicodemus in John 3. Staying within the perimeters of this Gospel to help us interpret the passage, we recognize that the author intends, or at least hopes, to lead the listener/reader to the belief that "Jesus is the Messiah, the Son of God, and that by believing you may have life in his name" (John 20:31). To accomplish this, the author uses various themes, one of them being darkness (unbelief / not knowing) and light (belief/knowing). The story of Nicodemus is right on the heels of the account of Jesus overturning the tables in the temple. The story following Nicodemus is the woman at the well. The historical and cultural backdrop is first-century CE Palestine. Nicodemus is a Pharisee and a member of the Jewish ruling council. It would be expected that he knows all things religious and holds a certain amount of political power, even though Rome is the occupying government. Culturally, he's the one who holds the answers to other people's questions. Geographically, the setting is Israel, and the time of day is nighttime. The passage tells us that Nicodemus has questions for Jesus. We can still stay true to the text even while we imaginatively weave these details into a story designed to help the listener identify with Nicodemus. My version is below. Your version, if you were creating the tale, would certainly be different.

Nicodemus tightly held his wrap around him. Usually, the breeze died down after the sun set, but not tonight. An unusual chill hung in the air. Nicodemus quickened his pace. His mind was troubled. The local gossip was buzzing about this young rabbi, Jesus. Nicodemus had heard about the episode at the temple, how Jesus had emptied the outer courts where the selling of animals suitable for ritual sacrifice took place. But Jesus had created quite a scene by overturning the tables at the money exchange booth. If the rabbi had a problem with temple business, certainly there was a better way to deal with it. When people had asked by what authority he was doing this, he made some delusional comment about rebuilding the temple in three days. Seriously? The elaborate temple had taken forty-six years to build.

Something was askew. It was Nicodemus's mission to get some clarification. After all, his position as one of the ruling council for the Jewish people demanded that he discover what was going on. Besides, he was extremely curious. He had observed Jesus interact with people. There was something intriguing about the way he somehow drew them in. It was obvious this young rabbi had a connection to God, even if he didn't have as much education or religious experience as Nicodemus had himself.

Nicodemus stumbled on the path. Walking through the streets in the dark could be challenging. He looked around, hoping no one saw him trip. That would be completely embarrassing, downright humiliating, for someone with his prestige and wisdom.

Nicodemus walked up the path toward the house where he was told that Jesus was staying. He heard voices in the enclosed yard, so he made his way to the gated opening. He was grateful for the enclosure. It was less likely that others would see him. He hoped his conversation with Jesus would shed some light on Jesus's behavior, as well as his teachings. Nicodemus craned his neck and looked into the yard. Jesus sat by the fire, chatting with his friends. Jesus paused his conversation and squinted at the shadowy figure who stood beyond the light of the fire.

In the imaginative version, I made several choices about the contexts I laid out. The climate of Israel often becomes chilly when the sun sets. I wondered about having Nicodemus be oblivious to the coolness because he was lost in his thoughts or possibly pointing out the chilly component to accentuate his discomfort. I also focused on Nicodemus's prestige and honor, which compounded his uneasiness, since he cannot claim to have answers and must instead sit in the discomfort of mystery. Admittedly, the answers that Nicodemus was given were confusing. I tossed in a stumble to amplify the sense of awkwardness and embarrassment and to heighten the sense of darkness.

Being mindful of multiple contextual components, I create a story that will help the listener connect with the character of the story and the distress that the character feels. If the listener can connect in those ways, I pray the listener will connect to the heart of the good news at the end of the story.

Throughout this chapter, we have considered various aspects of context. Each one has the potential to enrich a text. When we ignore the details embedded in the context, we are robbed of significant meaning held within the sacred texts. These elements enable the listener, as well as the reader, to relate with heart and mind to the character within the anecdote, keeping in mind that the ultimate goal is for the listener to encounter the Divine through the story. I suspect this was a significant goal for the authors of Scripture. May we partner with them and the Spirit of God to reach this same end.

4

Developing the Characters

My husband and I have three children. They are adults now and have children of their own. When they were younger, I studied them intently. Even as young preschoolers, each was unique. One was very quiet. Another was incredibly chatty. One was cautious. Another was adventurous. One enjoyed sweets. Another wanted "more meat" instead of dessert. (Who does that?) One could sit quietly. Another couldn't sit still enough to safely stay on the dining room chair for an entire meal.

One year shortly before Christmas, my husband suggested we give the older two children, ages six and four, a few dollars so they could buy Christmas presents for family members. It would be a good learning experience for them, requiring thoughtfulness and money management skills. I agreed, and we embarked on the escapade. With a toddler in the cart, we followed the two older children up and down the store aisles as they pondered the right gift for the right price for each person. With a little guidance, each one made their selections, and we made our way to the cashier where they paid for their purchases. One child had been intentional about each gift, being very focused on what the person might like and equally intent on keeping the price low. After paying for the gifts, he put the remaining cash in his pocket, thrilled at having money left over. The other child paid for the items he had selected, took the change he was given, and immediately walked over to the red kettle where the bell ringer stood. He then placed his last few coins through the slot on top of the container. Both children were happy with their decisions. These boys were brothers and yet very different from each other.

Personality Traits and Behavioral Styles

People are fascinating. I like watching them, observing their actions and interactions with others. Studying human temperaments, contemplating the inner workings of human beings, intrigues me. I continually wonder what drives people, what encourages them, and what gives each one a sense of fulfillment. Each person uniquely bears the image of God; each has proclivities in the ways they interact with the world, tendencies with strengths and weaknesses. Each individual strives to survive, and according to the Greek philosopher Plato, each one longs to find the good, the true, and the beautiful.

Our acquaintances display particular mannerisms. They might stand with their hands in their pockets or snort when they laugh at a funny joke. Our friends reveal their perspectives about life in their world. They chat about their employment, discuss the headlines of the news, or recount happenings of their recent vacation. Our family members and close friends divulge hopes and concerns for the present and the future. They share the disappointments about growing old or the struggles with being too young.

We recognize that the people in our lives have depth, with specific inclinations for the way they interact with their world. We are often drawn to people who have likes and dislikes similar to our own, behave in ways we can relate to, and share experiences comparable to ours. This is not to say that we aren't drawn to another person's differences; however, our ability to connect with others is directly impacted by their attributes and experiences.

When a preacher seeks to connect biblical characters to the listener of the sermon, it is essential to think about the characters' personality traits and behavioral styles. Allowing the people of Scripture to possess diverse characteristics enhances our ability to relate to them. As we begin to allow our imaginations concerning biblical witnesses to come alive, observing the people in our lives can be advantageous. The preacher doesn't need to be an expert on various personality or behavioral styles. Simply watching human beings can teach those of us who want to learn about these traits. Intentionally observing people and their behavior styles enables us to develop the tools necessary for wondering about the personality type of a biblical character.

Of course, human beings are complex. We have been shaped by a unique mix of experiences. We all have our own styles and exhibit a wide variety of traits. We display a range of emotions. All of these factors and many more create the people we are. Unraveling these components is a bit clunky, yet for the purposes of this book, I have chosen to focus on several common traits—behaviors, emotions and motivations, and intrinsic needs.

Observable Behavioral Traits

One significant quality to notice is a person's communication style. Does the individual communicate by making statements, or do they ask questions? Often, people who are talkative make statements. Persons who are less chatty are likely to ask questions. My husband and I were having dinner at our friends' house when the husband "asked" for the salt to be passed his direction. I chuckled to myself because he stated "I would like the salt" and finished with the tonal lilt of a question. His propensity toward communicating with statements was so prevalent that even when he tried to ask for the salt, he made a statement.

Another distinguishing characteristic is whether a person is motivated to do tasks or to spend time with people. Some individuals feel off-kilter if they haven't been with other people enough; their social quota needs to be filled. Others feel askew when their to-do list, which is always growing and never finished, remains untouched. They simply cannot relax or find pleasure in life without attending to their tasks. Returning to work one Monday, my husband asked his coworker if he had a good weekend. The colleague responded with a long list of accomplishments. He had chopped wood, mowed the lawn of his acreage, cleaned out the shed, and stained the deck. Then he concluded, "Yeah. It was a good weekend." Another friend of ours would have been disappointed with that type of weekend because it didn't include spending time with people or hosting a gathering for friends.

The nuances of personal disposition are many. Some people make decisions based on data, while others trust their guts. It is likely that the data-based decision makers cringed when they read the phrase "trust their guts." Some humans are optimists, seeing the positive and having hope for good people, good times, and good outcomes. Others are pessimists, holding their breath in anticipation of people behaving badly, the worst of times, and negative outcomes. (My experience is that pessimists claim to be realists.)

Being students of human nature gives our imaginations permission to apply these observations to persons within the pages of Scripture, assisting us in crafting believable characters. Is the individual within the story outgoing or reserved? Do they focus on accomplishing tasks, or do they linger with people? Do they follow a hunch, or do they collect copious amounts of information? How might the character rejuvenate? Is physical activity important to them? Would they rather attend a dinner party? Does a quiet walk, giving them time to think and ponder, restore their energy?

Using a behavioral assessment can enhance our imagination about how a character might function. Multiple assessments and tools are available to increase our knowledge. I often make reference to the DiSC assessment, due to my familiarity with the instrument. Myers-Briggs Type Indicator is another inventory for learning about personality preferences. Many other fascinating instruments exist for exploring and explaining personalities and behavioral traits. If a person wants to deepen their understanding, a brief exploration on the internet can inform them of some basic tenets of personality and behavior.

Thomas's Personality—Perhaps

The author of John's Gospel tells a story about Thomas (John 20:24–29). Through the years, I have heard many sermons on this passage concerning doubt and a possible lack of commitment on Thomas's part. When I was preparing to preach this passage, I started to imagine who Thomas might have been. By looking at other references to Thomas in the Gospel of John,

I realized that Thomas was deeply committed to Jesus. When Jesus prepares to go to Judea to be with Mary, Martha, and the soon-to-be risen Lazarus, the disciples are concerned. It hasn't been that long since the Jews tried to stone Jesus. Thomas is the one who says, "Let us also go, that we may die with him" (John 11:16). Thomas is prepared to die with Jesus. His commitment is strong.

Several chapters later, the unbelievable has happened. Jesus is alive after having been crucified and buried. The disciples marvel when they see Christ. But Thomas wasn't with them when Jesus made his appearance. Thomas insists, "Unless I see the nail marks in his hands and put my finger where the nails were, and put my hand into his side, I will not believe" (John 20:25). What if Thomas is an individual who needs more information, especially when asked to believe the unbelievable? Could it be that Thomas only wants to witness what the others have observed? And what if the purpose of the story isn't about scolding those who have doubts? Let's face it: we all doubt. Perhaps the purpose of the story is to convey amazement at a Christ who meets those who doubt right where they are. Imagining Thomas as a person who genuinely needs information and data in order to make decisions suggests a different understanding of the passage.

While I was doing my doctoral work, my relatives would occasionally ask me about the topic of my original research and thesis. One such conversation included sincere comments and questions rather than my personal monologue about my research. I shared my wonderings about Thomas. What if Thomas was allowed to be a person who needs data and information in order to come to good conclusions? This dear relative of mine abruptly stopped and stared at me. Then with wide eyes he said, "I'm that kind of person. I need data and information." Then he sighed, saying, "Sermons on that passage have always made me feel bad about myself." Imagining Thomas as a person who looks for significant amounts of data in order to make decisions gave my relative the possibility of identifying with Thomas's character. Consequently, he was able to wonder about the ways Christ is willing to connect with him.

Emotions and Motivations of the Character

Since the preacher is concerned with the spiritual realm of humanity, which in my experience is interwoven with the emotional dimension of humanity, developing the emotions and motivations of the witness within the scriptural narrative is vital. As humans, we have emotions. Feelings are an integral part of our personhood. Consequently, in order to shape a character in such a way that the listener can identify with them, the character's emotions must be developed. The emotional component aids the listener in empathizing with the person on the pages of Scripture.

As the preacher begins to imaginatively wonder about the character, it is important to consider what emotions the individual in the story might have. Once we begin to look for the character's feelings, we sometimes find mention of them. The woman who is subject to bleeding is "trembling with fear" (Mark 5:33). The disciples shriek "in fear" when they think Jesus is a ghost (Matt 14:26). The women leave the empty tomb "afraid yet filled with joy" (Matt 28:8). Zacchaeus welcomes Jesus "gladly" (Luke 19:6). When the disciples hear that James and John's mother asked for her sons to have positions of power in Jesus's kingdom, they are "indignant" (Matt 20:24). A Pharisee who is hosting

Jesus is "surprised" (Luke 11:38). These are only a few examples of an emotion being plainly stated.

At times, however, the tone of the sentiment is embedded in the passage. Jesus healed the woman who had been stooped over for eighteen years, and she "praised God" (Luke 13:13). While we can praise God even while we are grieving, in this situation, it isn't a stretch to imagine that the woman praised God in a joyful manner. The Gospels also tell us of Jesus's emotions. Jesus is angry in Mark 3:5. He has compassion for the people in Matthew 9:36, as well as many other passages. Jesus experiences joy in Luke 10:21.

In passages where the character's feelings are not mentioned, we have the freedom to imagine. There are many ways to go about this creative exercise, beginning by using yourself as information. How might you feel if you were in that person's shoes (hmmm, they likely wore sandals)? What are the things that keep you awake at night? Expand your viewpoint by thinking of others to whom you are close. What did you observe in your family of origin? How did your parent(s) express emotion? When a good friend received bad news, what kinds of feelings were expressed? All of us encounter similar foundational fears, such as the fear of isolation. The thought of being completely alone can cause our guts to twist and churn. Within our busy society, many of us long for some alone time to quiet our minds and our hearts. Yet thinking about being utterly alone and isolated, away from all those we love and who love us, causes our hearts to race.

The sense that we have value, while we each judge "value" according to different factors, compels us. Being cherished by someone somewhere impacts our psyches. Being shunned creates a painful imprint on our hearts. The fear of rejection and the desperation that accompanies such an experience drive many of us. Imprinted on our DNA is the need to be treasured. We seldom discuss the fact that our survival, our very ability to stay alive, depends on another person valuing our life. This valuing can have concrete ramifications. When human beings are not valued, their ability to obtain food and shelter is at risk. In more affluent societies, humans focus more on the psychological and spiritual need to be valued. We need to know and be known, love and be loved. We thrive when these needs are met. The absence of being known and being loved implies an absence of value, meaning we are expendable, disposable. Our life is without value. Being without value is another archetypal fear. While fear is an emotion, this "fear" is a motivation. It provokes us and often drives our behavior.

As the preacher begins imagining the emotions expressed in the biblical narrative, it is possible to limit the emotional expression so it always mirrors our own. Being intentional about the various fears and impulses we ascribe to a biblical character guards against our assuming they have the same feelings we do. In an effort to expand our thoughts about other's emotions, we might use a "feelings wheel" to explore various emotions. Another helpful tool is the Enneagram, which identifies nine types of human psyches. While it is a helpful tool for understanding personality traits, one of its unique features is that it identifies a base fear for each type. These fears are understood to be the driving motivations for a person's actions. A quick internet search can yield worthwhile information concerning archetypal fears that motivate us humans. We want to believe that we choose to behave a certain way because of its virtue, and maybe we sometimes do. But often, the impetus for our behavior is connected to assuaging our greatest fears. Our sense of who we need to be and what we need to do is motivated by our desire to be loved and accepted. For some, the thought that others would see them as selfish or stingy is problematic. For others, to be seen as careless or incompetent causes sleepless nights. Still others are anxious at being perceived as flippant or heartless. These concerns and more push us to behave in ways that we believe will cause the group to value us. Biblical characters experienced these concerns as well. Identifying the biblical character's central motivation helps that character come to life as we present their inner thoughts and fears.

As we consider what drives the characters in the narrative, let's go back to the Gospel of John. Both Thomas and Mary Magdalene are followers of Jesus. Yet Mary is at the foot of the cross and Thomas is not; Mary is at the grave and Thomas is not. What basic fear or desire might cause Mary Magdalene to remain in those places? What basic fear or desire might cause Thomas to not show up in those locations? Could Mary Magdalene be concerned that if she abandons Jesus, he will not know she loved him? What personal standard does Mary have that would be abolished if Jesus dies wondering about her love for him? Is she avoiding an overwhelming sense of guilt and shame she thinks she could feel if Jesus died without her by his side? Would she see herself as less valuable if she weren't there? Could Thomas be fraught with fear concerning his safety or, even greater, the safety of his family? What responsibilities does Thomas feel he must fulfill?

Creating characters who are motivated by their fears is essential. Fear and anxiety are central to human survival, and the listener can identify with such motivations. Note that the Gospel writers do not portray people as flawless. While our feelings are neither good nor bad, what we do as a result of our emotions may empower or paralyze us. Our desire to assuage our fundamental fears can drive us for good or for ill. The preacher might be tempted to minimize the fears that might motivate the characters of the sacred narrative. However, avoiding the development of almost-perfect people will be necessary to allow the listener to connect with the biblical witness. Few of us can relate to flawless persons.

I want to offer a word of caution. It is not my intent to overpsychologize the characters of Scripture. We are not participating in a Freudian analysis. We are simply identifying and describing archetypal longings and fears. All people struggle. This is part of being human. We experience heartache, grief, and pain. We muddle through times of being misunderstood and misrepresented. Our fear of rejection keeps us awake at night. Our concern for the state of our world robs us of a good night's sleep. The realization that we have little control in our lives, to say nothing of having even less control over the lives of those we love, weighs heavy on our hearts. Scripture repeatedly portrays God meeting biblical witnesses at their point of need. It is the preacher's responsibility to point to a Redeemer who cares about every aspect of our lives, including our thoughts and emotions. The overarching theme of the sacred narrative declares the Creator's divine faithfulness to the created. The preacher must proclaim the same.

Beyond the Obvious Needs

When we spend time reading and studying the Gospels, we read about Jesus's life, ministry, death, and resurrection. And while our faith tradition often emphasizes Jesus's crucifixion and the glorious resurrection, multiple chapters in all four Gospels recount his life and ministry, including his encounters with people who have physical, emotional, and spiritual needs. Many times, we point to these stories to consider what our behavior should be and how we ought to treat others. Yet we sometimes miss the fact that Jesus repeatedly met the needs of these individuals. Yes, we preach that Jesus fed the crowds, healed the sick, and cast out demons. Still, we often overlook the less visible, deeply personal needs that the people within the biblical narrative possessed. Many of the persons in the Gospels had presenting issues, such as health concerns or a need to be fed. These characters also had spiritual and emotional needs. In crafting a sermon that is relatable and easily accessible for today's listener, the preacher must acknowledge the people in the Holy Narrative had concerns similar to our own.

Maybe we don't preach about our deep needs because we are reluctant to acknowledge they exist. Many of the people I encounter display strength and prosperity. We seem to hide our worries and heartaches. Having it all together is respected. After all, success breeds success. Yet each person I know is carrying at least one burden, and sometimes multiple burdens, that weighs on them. Their heart aches. Their body refuses to cooperate. Their finances depreciate. Their relationships are fragile. Their mind spins. These are common human needs—needs for provision, relationship, and strength that all people since the beginning of time have experienced. Knowing that we are complete, interwoven, holistic beings, we can acknowledge that our physical needs impact our emotional needs. Our emotional needs are influenced by our spiritual needs. Our spiritual and psychological needs can be manifested in our physical bodies. Our needs are entangled. Our Western understanding looks at the parts to understand the whole. Yet this is limiting when we are considering our humanness. Yes, people consist of separate parts, *and* we are fully whole. This is also true of the characters in the biblical narrative. The struggle, then and now, is real.

Highlighting the less visible physical, emotional, and spiritual needs of the biblical witnesses creates the opportunity for the listener to empathize with the characters, as well as to recognize their own need within the story. Allowing a character to feel hopeless, frantic, or lonely creates an opening for the hearer to encounter the Divine. As we again imagine the situation for the man born blind (John 9), we can surmise that due to his physical blindness, he experienced other psychological wounds, such as separation, loneliness, and rejection. In the first century CE, those with physical challenges would have been kept on the outside of society. They were not considered valuable and were forced to the fringes. (Two thousand years later, our culture has taken only small steps toward seeing someone with physical limitations as a meaningful contributor to society.) Is it possible that the man born blind longed to be included? Did he dream about going to the temple for the festivals? Yearning for inclusion is a common human desire. After being healed, the blind man found himself before the Pharisees. This interaction was a debacle, and the man was thrown out and excommunicated. The healed man once again found himself on the outside.

Imagining that the man in John 9 is lonely and longing to be included prepares us to hear the words of John 9:35: "Jesus heard that they had thrown him out, and when he found him . . ." The phrase "and when he found him" acknowledges that Jesus went looking for the man. Jesus sought out the man who longed to be included. Then Jesus asked him, "Do you believe in the Son of Man?" Keep in mind that in the Gospel of John, the word *believing* is not about giving mental assent as much as it is about being in relationship. Jesus offers the man an opportunity to belong with him. The man who has a need to be included is included by the Loving Includer. Carefully portraying the man's longing—his loneliness, a universal human desire—allows Christ to meet this universal human desire, both for the man in the story and for the listener.

When we look at the various characters in the stories of Scripture, we must acknowledge they were fully human with multiple needs. Thus as we craft the story for preaching, we need to acknowledge the emotional needs of the character. We might ask, for example, In what ways does Jesus meet an emotional and spiritual need in an individual's life? How do the feedings or healings or casting out of demons affect the psychological need of the person in the story? By attending to such needs, we will construct space for the listener, with their various needs, to encounter the Divine.

Yes, the stories shared in the Gospels tell of people who have presenting issues—problems such as a physical illness or disease—or the chief concern might be feeding a multitude. I wonder if we have fixated on Jesus meeting the presenting needs and have missed the fact that he attends to other needs of the biblical characters, including those that are emotional, psychological, and spiritual. As an example, Mark 5:25–34 tells us of the woman who was "subject to bleeding for twelve years." Jesus tells her following her healing that her faith has healed her. Her faith pushes her to take action. She goes to where Jesus is. She reaches out and touches Jesus's cloak. She is healed. And through the healing encounter with Jesus, he meets her deep, foundational fears—the fears of being isolated, or not having value, or not being loved or lovable—that connect her to all humankind.

Certainly, this story is meant to impact people who aren't "subject to bleeding." Physically, she is struggling; plus, her bleeding informs the reader that religiously and culturally she is considered unclean (Lev 15:25–26). Being unclean likely requires her to stay at home, and she certainly isn't permitted to go to the temple. The emotional and psychological burdens of being considered unclean for twelve years, and possibly being homebound and isolated from much of her society, are bound to have an impact on her. Physically, since she is "subject to bleeding," her ability to procreate is likely in question. This would be devastating in a culture where women are considered blessed if they have children and where a woman's value is directly connected to having offspring. It stands to reason that this woman likely does not have a sense of being valued.

The author of Mark tells us that even though Jesus is on his way to an important man's house (to heal his daughter—hmmm, another reinforcement that females are important to God, even in a culture that placed little value on women), when he realizes "that power had gone out from him" (Mark 5:30), he stops to see who touched him. The disciples insist that it isn't that important. But Jesus keeps looking for the person. The woman is fearful. Why would she be fearful? Could it be that she is supposed to be at home? Has she decided that she has no value? But Jesus keeps looking. When she comes forward, he listens to the whole story. Then he addresses her as "daughter" (v. 34). Notice, too, that Jesus says, "Go in peace and be freed from your suffering" (v. 34). Peace is a sense of well-being, an emotional and a spiritual state. Certainly, her suffering was more than simply physical. Throughout the saga, Jesus continues to confer value on the woman. He assuages her deep fear of having no value, of being a disposable person.

Such reflection on the story causes us to listen for ways in which Christ confers value on us. Does Christ keep looking for us? Might the Spirit listen to our whole story? Could it be that the Divine calls us by a familial title, a designation of belonging? Interacting with the Holy Narrative, again, proves to be rich and filled with meaning! We dare not minimize the lavish depth of Scripture by leaving the text and its characters as lifeless caricatures. We must acknowledge the fears and desires, concerns and needs, that Christ is longing to meet.

The Character's Mind

As human beings, our minds are busy. We spend time thinking, pondering, and giving meaning to happenings in our lives—activities of our conscious minds. But even so, we have more to process; consequently, as we sleep, our minds continue working. When we remember an occurrence, we may attempt to better understand the recollection. We wonder about things we know and things we don't know. Our thoughts can be productive and enrich our lives, and they can spin in tireless spirals, holding us captive in unhealthy ways. Biblical characters, since they are human beings, also have active minds. While we don't want to go too deeply into the workings of a character's mind (I discuss this in the next chapter), the preacher can utilize a character's thoughts, memories, and wonderings to communicate a variety of informative details, such as cultural norms or religious expectations, without simply stating the information. This technique is helpful in engaging the listener.

Let's explore Mark 3:1–6. Jesus goes to the local synagogue on the Sabbath and sees a man with a lame hand. Jesus already has a reputation for healing people and not placing a high enough priority on the religious laws; consequently, the religious leaders are watching the situation closely. Verse 3 states, "Jesus said to the man with the shriveled hand, 'Stand up in front of everyone.'" What do you think ran through the mind of the man with the lame hand? What cultural norms and religious expectations could be communicated by exploring the man's thoughts? Here's what I have imagined:

> The man dropped his chin to his chest and stared at his feet. His mind was racing. Excitement and trepidation flooded him. He knew that Jesus healed people. Maybe today that would happen for him. But the man also knew that today was the Sabbath, that there were restrictions about working on a holy day, and that the religious leaders protected the religious law with vigor. He respected their zeal for God, and he didn't want to be in the middle of this argument. The man appreciated the challenging spot the religious leaders were in. The Romans didn't respect the Jewish people, their religion, or their religious laws. And now this young rabbi, instead of protecting and adhering to the religious law, had a reputation for also being a bit cavalier about their traditions. And yet there was something intriguing about this young rabbi. To hear him talk about God made the man long to know God in such a meaningful way. The man's thoughts continued to spin while everyone watched him. He didn't want or need this attention, but he wanted to be healed. If his lame hand was fully restored . . . oh, the possibilities!

Utilizing the man's thoughts can allow the preacher to explain the cultural context while creating a connection between the man and the listener.

Thoughts also take the form of memories. As humans, we are connected deeply to our memories. Our recollection of past events can shape how we understand the world and help form our identities. We employ our experiences to solve problems. Our memories may be intentionally recalled or a knee-jerk reaction to various situations. It's not unusual to engage our memories when making decisions. Our relationships are also impacted by the ways we perceive past occurrences. Let's face it: we are our memories. Our ability to recall our past, whether short term or long term, is so significant that we fear losing this cognitive ability.

The characters in Scripture also had memories. Referring to the character's memories is another way to add depth to the biblical witness, enhancing the listener's ability to identify with them. Recollection also can honor the scriptural context. (Yes, we're back to context.) In our recounting, the biblical witness can "remember" events that led up to the text of the sermon. This recalling can be used to enhance the understanding of the passage's literary context. When working within the Gospels, it is appropriate to ask what the author has written earlier in that particular Gospel. For example, in Matthew 19:13–15, we read of Jesus instructing the disciples to let the children come to him and blessing them. What might James and John think about that situation? Keeping the story in the context of Matthew's Gospel, remember that a couple of chapters before Jesus blesses the children, he was transformed on the mountain and in conversation with Moses and Elijah. James and John observed that event. If they understood Jesus's transformation as a sign of power, what kind of dissonance might have been created within their minds when he blesses children, the little ones who are low in the cultural hierarchy of the day? What memories of the transfiguration could be expressed when they see Jesus blessing the children? Are they dumbfounded to see Jesus, the one who visits with Moses and Elijah—those great faith leaders—now placing value on little ones? Do James and John wonder if they have misunderstood power and its purpose?

Continuing in this manner, Matthew 20:20–28 tells us of James and John's mother asking if her two sons could have roles of power and prestige within Christ's kingdom. When the other ten hear about it, the situation becomes heated. Jesus uses the episode as a teaching moment. How might James and John hear Jesus's comments with the previous stories in mind (blessing the children and the transfiguration)? Utilizing the character's memories can enhance the meaning of the story.

Extending grace to the biblical witnesses is imperative. Throughout the Gospels, Jesus is revealing the Divine to the people he encounters. The learning curve is steep for them, just as it is for us when our theological understanding is disturbed by a new insight, experience, or piece of information. We, as finite human beings, are not capable of comprehending the Infinite One. We try . . . and we cannot fully grasp the Life Sustainer who is beyond our understanding. The characters of Scripture wonder and muse about the Divine. Some of their deliberations are recorded for us (Luke 2:19; John 3:1–15; etc.). As characters of Scripture are developed, the preacher can implement the characters' wonderings to point the listener toward the central theme of the sermon.

What kind of wonderings might the woman in Luke 7:36–50 entertain? Jesus is dining at a Pharisee's house when a woman with a bad reputation shows up. She comes because she has heard Jesus is there. Her tears are enough to wet his feet. She proceeds to wipe his feet with her hair, kisses them, and pours perfume on them. What might she be wondering? Does she wonder if Jesus will recoil? Does she wonder if Jesus truly knows about her life? Does she wonder if love and forgiveness will be extended to her? A sermon using this passage and focusing on the theme of the love and forgiveness of the Redeemer might explore our own wonderings and concerns that we might not be loved or forgiven. Can we make ourselves fully vulnerable to the Divine, confessing all our wrong choices, our selfish motives, our arrogant judgments, our cravings for power? Will we be met with forgiveness and peace?

Supporting Characters

Up until now, I've discussed the story from the perspective of the main character of the vignette. However, looking at a scene through another character's eyes can also enrich a passage. Other characters are often mentioned in the sagas recounted for us in the Gospels. Life experience has taught us that the happenings in another's life impact a great number of people. While we, as Americans, value individualism, we know that we are all connected to one other—a truth that applies to scriptural stories as well. When a person encounters Jesus within the Gospel narratives, that meeting ripples out to other people. And each person touched by the encounter perceives it in their own way.

In considering the story of Jesus walking on the water, the author of Matthew depicts Peter as a key character (Matt 14:22–33). Yet many other disciples are in the boat. What might this experience have been like for James, who grew up in a family of fishers (Matt 4:21)? What was he thinking and feeling during the night on the water? What might have crossed his mind when Peter proposed he join Jesus on the water? Which of Jesus's words did James hear? What emotions might he have felt when Peter was outside of the boat?

Ponder the story of James and John's mother asking for her sons to be granted privileged and powerful positions (Matt 20:20–28). The text includes the other ten disciples and tells us they were "indignant" when they heard of this. What caused the other ten to have this emotional response? What meaning did they give the mother's request? The situation had implications for each of the ten. What repercussions existed for them? The stories within the sacred narratives are filled with supporting characters who are specifically named as individuals or as groups. Exploring their perspectives can be meaningful.

While imagining the tale from another's viewpoint can enhance a story with which we are quite familiar, it may also allow the listener to find themselves in the story. At times, a supporting character's role and experience might be an easier way for the listener to connect. For some, the idea of being the main character is uncomfortable. Different people have different ways of interacting with life. Some charge ahead; others watch for a while before joining in. Some move faster; others move slower. Some make quick decisions; others take time to decide. For those who are more likely to be observers, a supporting character in the scene might be more relatable. Giving the listener the opportunity to identify with characters in the sacred narrative by including the perspective of a supporting character might help them find themselves within the story.

As we wrestle with biblical stories, we can assume there are characters in the saga who are not mentioned in the passage. We can remain true to the text and context while allowing our imaginations to include these characters in the narrative. Again, we don't make claims that contradict Scripture. *And* . . . we know that each person has a mother. Many are fortunate to have siblings and other relatives. If one has a job, they are likely to have a supervisor. If the character owns a business, they likely have family working with them. Who isn't in the pages of Scripture but might have been a part of the tale?

The anecdote of Jesus turning water into wine provides a good example. In John 2, the author tells us of multiple characters: Jesus's mother, Jesus, the disciples, the servants, the master of the banquet, and the bridegroom. The implied characters would include guests, family members, and the *bride*. Numerous perspectives from various viewpoints, named and unnamed, are available in this story. In a sermon I preached to denominational leaders and pastors, I took great liberty and imagined a head servant in the account. I imagined that the servant had been making plans for weeks. He (in Jesus's culture, a person with that much responsibility would likely have been male) would have been responsible for every detail of the celebration and how well it went. How would the head servant have felt when they ran out of wine? Did his head spin as he tried to figure out why this had happened? Was he concerned that his master would blame him? What ramifications would there have been for running out of wine? For him? For the bridegroom? Plans had been made. Extensive work had been done. And now there was no more wine. Jesus's instructions for correcting the situation—filling six stone water jars—would have required a great deal of additional labor. And when the servants were done with that task, the head servant might have reasonably assumed they would still have only water. All that hard work and still no wine. Let's not forget, it was Jesus who turned the water into wine.

By injecting a head servant into the story, I created a person who was responsible for the details of the wedding celebration and who worked hard for his master. Then I could easily move from the imagined story to wondering about times when we make plans and work hard—sometimes, perhaps often, with little confidence in the outcome. The denominational leaders and pastors could effortlessly recognize the extensive work they were doing for the church. I then circled around to the truth that regardless of our hard work and ongoing effort, we need Christ to turn our water into wine.

Wondering who the peripheral characters are—those who are listed and not listed in a passage—and pondering their experiences, their feelings, and their thoughts can enrich the stories we find in the sacred Scriptures. Even if we do not utilize the supporting characters' imagined experiences, the exercise is likely to influence the sermon we preach. Allowing Scripture and its characters to come alive brings nuances to the forefront and enriches the Holy Narrative.

Including the Epistles

To this point, I have explored only Gospel texts, which are full of stories that reveal who God is and Christ's remarkable transforming power. However, the imaginative storytelling style can be adapted to work with the Epistles. The Epistles, though they are not filled with stories, transpire within a narrative. The authors and the original audiences lived a story. The traditional understanding of each letter's authorship (and yes, I acknowledge there are well-thought-out arguments for the possibility that the authors are different from those traditionally presumed) can be helpful as we allow our imaginations to create a setting for the letter. Throughout the Gospels and the book of Acts, we learn about those who are believed to have written the Epistles. These details are good starting places for shaping the imagined backstory for these writings.

When we are working with a story within one of the Gospels, I contend that the preacher should stay within the literary confines of that particular Gospel rather than importing details from the other Gospels. Each Gospel was written with its own purpose and for its own audience. Some of the Epistles were similarly targeted. Philemon was addressed only to Philemon, Apphia, and Archippus plus the church that met in their home (Phlm 1:1–2). The audience of Philemon was specific, as is the story contained in that letter. When we preach from the Epistles, however, we should keep in mind that while aspects of some letters were aimed at one audience, many of these letters were shared among various churches, and the audience was intended to be broad. Galatians is an example of an Epistle intended for a more expansive group—"the churches in Galatia" (Gal 1:2).

Acknowledging a broader audience for some Epistles grants us permission to shape the narrative of the texts by using other sacred passages that inform us about an author or a letter's events and audience. For example, Paul is credited with authoring the letter to "God's holy people in Ephesus" (Eph 1:1). Knowing some of the backstory about Paul's connections with this community found in Acts 18:19–21, I could imagine the setting of a text in Ephesians. The Ephesian elders' love for Paul was immense. Paul had worked side by side with them, teaching them, caring for them, and encouraging them. How might that knowledge impact our understanding of the tone of Paul's comments?

Years ago, in order to expand my own experience with these imaginative storytelling sermons, I decided to wade into a passage from one of the Epistles. The Revised Common Lectionary assigned 2 Corinthians 12:2–10 for that particular Sunday. In keeping with the tradition that Paul is the author, holding in mind the topics covered before chapter 12, and drawing on the backdrop of the story in Acts 18, I began imagining Paul pacing back and forth as he dictated to a scribe or personal secretary who was writing the letter. In my imagination, the secretary reads topics back to Paul to remind him of what he has covered. Paul and the scribe talk about Paul's love for these people and his frustration with their discrediting his ministry. Going through this exercise changed my perspective of Paul. I had understood the apostle Paul as a harsh authoritarian with little respect for anyone who understood the world differently from the way he did. Imagining Paul's conversation with his personal secretary caused me to have empathy for him. Earlier, I had read a severe tone of voice into his writings. Now his nature and his comments were less harsh and even gentle at times. While I had related to characters in the Gospels this way, I had never encountered Paul in this manner. Experiencing Paul as a human being permitted me to hear some of his teachings in a more meaningful way.

Gracious Limits

The methodology of biblical imagination can also be utilized with the stories of the Hebrew Scriptures. The preacher needs to have a solid understanding of the historical and cultural context of the time period, as well as Jewish customs. The writings and teachings of Old Testament scholars can enrich the preacher's understanding of these considerations. It is imperative that Christian preachers, when speaking from the Hebrew Scriptures, honor Jewish traditions and consider the original intent of the narrative.

No matter what part of the canon we focus on in a sermon, when we use our imaginations to engage with the Holy Narrative, we must be true to the context of Scripture. We must honor the historical and cultural framework in which the passages are set. There are limits. But as is often true of limits, these perimeters enrich the process and enliven the Word. And yet . . . we have incredible freedom to imagine the characters of Scripture as real people living in a real time and having real needs as they encounter a real God.

Being true to Scripture requires us to acknowledge that the characters in the narrative are human beings, and it is crucial we allow them to be so much more than one-dimensional caricatures. It is not my goal to suggest that preachers articulate every aspect of human emotions, concerns, and motivations. Yet intentionally developing characters to enhance their relatability for the listener will certainly be beneficial. As we deepen our portrayal of these biblical witnesses, probing their humanness—their personalities, behavioral traits, emotions, motivations, and needs—we find Christ responding to the yearnings of their souls and ours. This is the good news: Christ meets us in all our needs. This is where transformation takes place. When we preach in such a way that the listener can encounter the Lover of our Souls through Scripture, we are partnering with the Living Word to fulfill the purpose of these precious texts that have been preserved for us through the ages. Of course, as we allow our imaginations to swell with possibilities of a richer character portrayal, it is important to stay true to Scripture. Our description of a character cannot contradict Scripture. And yet there is a vast amount of wiggle room. May we dance and play with the Spirit, may our hearts be rejuvenated, and may we sink deeper into the Divine as we grapple with these incredible texts.

5

Visualizing the Narrative

Years ago at an Easter service, I experimented with a first-person story. I eagerly shared the story and the promise of new life as if I were Mary Magdalene. At the close of the service, congregation members filed out the door, shaking my hand as they went. One person confessed, "I couldn't figure out who was talking sometimes. Was it you or Mary Magdalene?" My attempt had caused confusion and fallen flat for at least one listener. I wondered how many others had struggled as well.

In the previous chapter, we explored ways to imagine the experiences of the main human character as well as supporting characters in the biblical narratives. (The Divine is always the *main* character.) As preachers, we need to see ourselves in the characters of the narrative. Identifying with characters by connecting with their emotions, needs, and concerns, we discover their desires are our desires. When we relate to the characters, we can empower the listener to find their place within the biblical saga. Yet this storytelling need not be a first-person account.

What the Narrator Observes

Sharing the story as a narrator—as an outside observer who sees what is happening—has great merit. Paul Scott Wilson, a preaching professor and author, advocates thinking of a sermon in much the same way a filmmaker would visualize a scene.[1] A film, whether intended for the small screen or the big screen, communicates without words. What can be *seen* speaks volumes. Similarly, when allowing the imagination to visualize a tale, the story often has a greater impact on the listener. Describing aspects of the setting, the environment in which the saga takes place, enables the hearer to envision the story as it unfolds in their mind. But there is so much more to see than just the setting. Since many people are visual learners and communicators (thus the truth of the saying "A picture's worth a thousand words"), the sermon will likely hold more of the listener's attention when the preacher answers the question, "What else can we see?" As we imagine a biblical narrative within its historical and cultural setting, as well as learn from the text itself, we can observe and describe many details. In our telling, we provide the opportunity for listeners to "see" the scene for themselves.

A character's appearance and other details can be revealing. Let's use Zacchaeus as an example. Luke 19:2–3 reports that Zacchaeus was a chief tax collector, wealthy, and short in stature. The preacher could state those descriptors and offer some historical explanation about what it meant to be a tax collector and why tax collectors were wealthy. The preacher could also comment on Zacchaeus's height disadvantage. Or a preacher could describe what an observer would see and thus encourage the listener to visualize the scene. Here is an example:

Zacchaeus gripped his flowing robe in his right fist, each finger adorned with a ring. As he held the robe close to his body, he looked around at the crowd of commoners. He curled his lip, wrinkling his nose. He didn't want his embroidered robe to get soiled as he ran along the edge of the crowd, although there was little chance that he would get close enough to any of the bystanders. People in the crowd stepped out of his way, not as a courtesy, but with disdain etched on their faces. Tax collectors were traitors, and Zacchaeus was no exception.

He wasn't accustomed to running. People in his position did not engage in such behavior. It was beneath their status. Yet Zacchaeus's feet moved quickly. He didn't care what they thought. He was trying to get a glimpse of Jesus. Each time he stopped to catch his breath, he stood on his tiptoes, wondering if he could see Jesus.

This same technique can be used to envision a beggar. What descriptions might be shared from the perspective of an observer that might imply a person's desperate economic plight? What kind of clothing would a beggar wear? Is the fabric threadbare or tattered?

Physical maladies can be visible. Several stories in the Gospels involve people who have a skin disease, often referred to as leprosy. Skin diseases frequently produce visible sores. What might be observable from the viewpoint of an onlooker? Are the lesions oozing? Have some wounds scabbed over? We need not go overboard, yet the description of the festering sores enhances the astonishment of bystanders when Jesus touches the man with leprosy in Matthew 8:1–3. Other conditions might not be visible, yet descriptions of symptoms can still be beneficial. For example, when Peter's mother-in-law had a fever (Matt 8:14), were her cheeks flushed? Was her hair matted to her forehead due to sweat? Did Peter's wife place her hand on her mother's forehead? Describing what is visible about the character can hold the listener's attention and allow them to see the scene and its many implicit nuances.

Letting the Listener See the Emotion and Thoughts

In the previous chapter, I discussed the importance of capturing the emotions of the characters in the biblical narrative. We might think emotions are difficult to observe, yet many of us are attuned to other people's emotions and do not need to be told what a person is feeling. Humans communicate a great deal with facial expressions. Is a person's brow furrowed? Are the eyebrows scrunched toward each other or raised in an arch? Are the eyes opened wide, or is the person squinting? Is the person biting their lip as their chin quivers? Are the corners of the mouth slowly turning upward? Emotions are communicated in all these facial expressions.

A person's body language also suggests their emotional state. Are they holding their head in their hands? Are their hands clenched into fists? Are their shoulders thrust back and their head held high as they walk? Is their stride brisk or leisurely? Is the character kicking their toe in the dirt? As the preacher describes what is seen by the imaginative eye, the listener has the freedom to conclude which emotional response might be occurring for the character. These images may lead listeners to different meanings, yet these conclusions are more likely to allow listeners to identify with the individual in Scripture, connecting their own experiences and emotions to those of the character.

Let's wonder together about Peter when Jesus asks him for the third time, "Do you love me?" The passage says that Peter was "hurt" (John 21:17). What body language might Peter display? What happens with his shoulders? Does he cross his arms? Does he begin cracking his knuckles? Does he kick at the pebbles on the seashore? In what direction is he gazing? Is he looking at the ground? Is he staring beyond Jesus? The preacher can provide clues about the emotional experience of the character. Describing their actions gives the listener the opportunity to discern the emotion of the character.

Thoughts can also be communicated by action. Anyone who has spent time with children knows this firsthand—the hands clapping at a piece of good news, the eye roll, the refusal to make eye contact, the audible sigh. Communication is much more complex than simply using words.

Let's work with the teaching of Jesus traditionally called the Sermon on the Mount. Jesus is teaching his disciples and continues to expand concepts they had previously been taught. When we humans learn ideas and beliefs that expand what we have formerly trusted, we feel unsettled. With this knowledge of human behavior, we can begin to wonder what it might have been like for the disciples as they listened to Jesus's sermon. When Jesus told the crowd to turn the other cheek (Matt 5:38–39), what facial expressions might a narrator observe? Did Andrew's eyes open wide? Did he tilt his head to the side? Did James's and John's eyes meet, creating a telling exchange? Were their eyebrows raised? When Jesus continued by teaching that they should love their enemies (Matt 5:43–47), did Peter cross his arms, purse his lips, and furrow his brow? These teachings are challenging to those of us who have heard them for years; imagine how perplexing they might have been for the disciples who were hearing them for the first time.

Describing facial expressions and body language can be an effective way to communicate cultural norms. When something transpires in the story that would have been abnormal for the culture or worldview of the players in the narrative, assuredly there was a reaction. As an observer of the imagined story, what do you see?

As an example, let's once again consider Luke 19:1–10. When Jesus reached the tree that held the tax-collecting traitor named Zacchaeus, those who heard Jesus say that he was going to stay at Zacchaeus's house likely communicated their thoughts and emotions with their faces and bodies. The cultural and religious expectation was that "good people" did not extend hospitality to or accept it from such "sinners." According to verse 7, people in the crowd grumbled about Jesus's declaration that he would stay at Zacchaeus's house. What did that look like? Did they turn their backs to Jesus as they complained to one another about Jesus's plan? Did they whisper, or did they speak just loudly enough for Jesus to hear their aghast reaction? Could it be that the disciples themselves took a physical step back when they heard Jesus's intentions? What microexpressions filled the faces of the people and the disciples who were nearby? Allowing our imaginations to picture what these interactions looked like will enhance our ability to describe the scene for the listener. As we ponder these details of the interaction between Jesus and Zacchaeus, the implication of Jesus's accepting Zacchaeus's hospitality deepens and invites the listener to relate to a life-transforming experience with the Divine.

A Visible Story of a Verbal Teaching

Capturing and conveying a passage has two components. One aspect is describing the detail and action of the characters specifically mentioned in the passage. The other is to portray the imaginative aspects of the story, some of which display the emotional experiences and thoughts of the characters. When there is action in the passage, depicting what is visible might seem more feasible. So how do we create a visible story of a verbal teaching?

Again, context matters. Within the Gospels, the authors share with the reader who the audience is and what has occurred leading up to Jesus's teaching. Although the Gospels are not arranged in chronological order, the authors have been intentional about the placement of stories and teachings within their accounts. The stories and teachings inform each other throughout each book. Utilizing this information, the preacher can deduce a possible intent of the author and begin creating the scene. We first gather details, then proceed to our imaginative activity. What does Scripture tell us concerning who is listening? Where might this teaching be taking place? What happened prior to this teaching? How do those details impact the teaching? Then we transition to wondering how this teaching is being received by the listeners. What might their facial expressions be? What might their body language tell us?

Let's work with the good shepherd discourse in John 10. Jesus is using a shepherd and sheep metaphor. In the previous chapter, the Pharisees are actively involved in the saga. They scrutinize the account shared by the man who used to be blind, and they take offense at Jesus's comments. Jesus directly addresses the Pharisees in verse 1, and verse 6 tells us they do not understand. With this information, the preacher could imagine the expressions on the

Pharisees' faces. What do their body movements convey about the emotions of their hearts?

Another way to deal with this passage might be to reflect on the two groups of Jews who are present. According to verses 19–21, the people are divided. Some think Jesus is demon possessed; others refute that conclusion. What expressions might be visible on the faces of the people who are impressed with the healing of the blind man? Are they occasionally nodding their heads? Do they look heavenward as they ponder Jesus's words? Are they focused on Jesus and leaning forward to hear more? Do some take deep, slow breaths and exhale, letting their shoulders fall? The second group also displays expressions through their faces and bodies. Are their lips pursed? Are they gritting their teeth? What are their eyebrows doing? Are some clenching their fists? Are others wringing their hands? How are they breathing? Are their breaths quick and shallow? By interspersing these visible expressions, the preacher can add a thoughtful dimension to the message, helping today's listener engage with Jesus's teaching. While most descriptions should have a definitive purpose, not all facial expressions and aspects of body language will be defined. This is true in our lives too. Some descriptions will resonate with some listeners in a variety of ways. The listener is likely to connect with the visible expression that matches their experience.

Allowing our imaginations to play with the details found in the narrative can help shape the scene in our minds as preachers and then in the mind's eye of the listener. By creating a picture of the place and time that the listener can grasp, we have the potential for making a greater impact within the heart of the hearer. The goal of visually telling the story is to create space within the listener's mind and heart so that they can be impacted by connecting with Jesus. This is much more than merely expanding knowledge of Jesus's teachings. When Jesus declares that the greatest commandment is to "love the Lord your God with all your heart and with all your soul and with all your mind" (Matt 22:37), he invites us into a relationship, a connection, a life-changing I'm-all-in commitment that includes, and yet goes far beyond, our intellect. As we engage with, grapple with, and ponder the stories of Scripture, may these Holy Narratives impact our whole being.

6

Encountering God

Days of playing hard and being out of a daily routine had caught up with our granddaughters. But that's exactly what is supposed to happen when granddaughters and grandparents spend several days together. Bedtimes are later than usual. Schedules and eating habits are altered. Activity, fun, junk food, and making memories are the priorities. But these types of decisions have consequences. The exhaustion, poor eating, and upheaval of an orderly life culminated in a challenging bedtime that night. Simple tasks—putting on their pajamas and brushing their teeth—were met with pouting and tears, followed by a refusal to crawl into bed. The only ones to blame for this episode were the grandparents. We had offered too many sweets and ignored good routines. The sweet cherubs finally acquiesced amid stern instructions and laid their heads on their pillows with sniffling pleas for a bedtime story. Not wanting the day to end on a sour note, I consented. I was too tired to create a fanciful tale, so I went for the obvious. I put the day's activities into a story.

I began, "Once upon a time, there were two little girls who were very much loved by their grandparents. Everyone was happy that they could spend time together. One day they went to the park together, and they climbed on the equipment and slid down the slide, and their grandpa and grandma pushed them in the swings. And those two little girls knew that their grandparents loved them very much." I continued listing the activities we had enjoyed throughout the day: walking and skipping around the block, having lunch at our favorite fast-food joint, learning about reptiles at the local reptile zoo, playing a board game, roasting hot dogs and marshmallows over a fire, and getting ready for bed. After describing each activity, I repeated the mantra "And those two little girls knew that their grandparents loved them very much." With the final reminder of the grandparents' love, I pronounced, "The end." To which my oldest granddaughter replied, "Aw, Grams. That story's like us." I smiled, leaned over and kissed her forehead, said goodnight, and left the room, stifling my giggle. The story wasn't "*like* us." It *was* us!

The Story Is Ours

Often, I fear, we have a similar misunderstanding when we approach Scripture. We marvel at the stories. We think about the narrative. We contemplate the concepts. We slice and dice the possible meanings. And all the while, we are missing that the stories of Scripture are *our* stories. We—as humans, with all our needs and desires, disappointments and losses, joys and delights, missteps and failures—are intertwined with the characters of the Holy Narrative. As we embrace the truth that all humans throughout time have comparable needs, we can begin to grasp the reason preachers need to empower listeners to find themselves within these sacred tales. Yet many of us have been trained, whether intentionally or unintentionally, to focus on the so-called objective claims of Scripture and steer away from the subjective lens of imagination. Charles Denison—author, speaker, and Presbyterian pastor—wrote in his book *The Artist's Way of Preaching*, "Objectivity is scientific, rational, and left-brained. Objectivity is boring. Objectivity is by definition impersonal. Give us the personal!"[1]

From my observations, our society values the scientific method for comprehending both the enormity and the microscopic aspects of the cosmos. I am ever so grateful for this approach, especially when my health is involved or we are sending people into outer space or technology is being formed or electricity is made available. Praise be to God for a scientific methodology. Yet treating the holy texts with a scientific protocol, stripping them of the personal and viewing them as simply information and data, starves our souls and hinders our spiritual development. Many people have shared with me that they hunger for a different style and attitude concerning Scripture, one with which they can identify and that offers a deeper spiritual connection. When we as preachers recognize how our fully human story is represented in the stories of fully human characters within the texts, our sermons will in turn invite the listeners to find themselves within the divine story line.

As I have stood in the back of the sanctuary, shaking hands with church attendees as they exit the service, I have heard various comments about preaching biblical characters—comments of appreciation for holding a person's attention, remarks of genuine connection with the story, and amazement at a fresh way of looking at the holy text. Allowing characters to become multidimensional people can be impactful for the listener, yet not everyone resonates with a storytelling style. When speaking at a preaching workshop, I shared some of the data from my research (see chapter 1) acknowledging that 17 percent of the participants who were surveyed did not find stories to be a useful source of learning. One of the preachers attending the workshop raised his hand and blurted out before I could even acknowledge him, "I doubt that. We all learn from stories." I chuckled aloud, shrugged my shoulders, and continued to point to the empirical data from the small pool of people who had been surveyed. Yet I suspect that preacher might have been right.

Once, a Sunday school teacher excitedly shared with me that one week, she decided to try an interactive method of teaching the lesson. She encouraged her students to imagine performing a television interview with a biblical character. She had special hats and glasses and scarves and necklaces for the students to use as props as they role-played. These elementary-age students were fully participating and learning their lesson that particular Sunday. I suspect that many of us, even as adults, would have been equally involved. Many adults enjoy using their imaginations. My experience indicates that a sermon that occupies the imagination of the listener will often cause children, teens, and adults to be fully engaged. The research for my project confirms that conclusion, as do several encounters that I have had the delight of experiencing.

While we intellectually understand, and possibly even agree with, the importance of telling the stories of Scripture, preaching a different style of sermon can be nerve-wracking. We like to use our tried-and-true methods, and our congregations have certain expectations. As preachers and pastors, we often feel a responsibility to meet the expectations that others have for us. Stepping out of our comfort zone—and maybe the congregation's—can heighten our anxiety. With this in mind, I'd like to provide some encouragement by telling a couple of stories related to the research I did for my doctor of ministry dissertation.

Before and After

Collecting data from others' experiences would be necessary in order for me to understand how this imaginative storytelling sermon style impacts listeners. My research for my doctoral project included a group of people who agreed to listen to four sermons that I would preach. I would craft these sermons utilizing my imagination to enhance the story in the text. I planned to explore behavioral styles and archetypal fears (as described earlier in this book) to develop characters with whom the listeners could identify. Some of the participants were members of my congregation and had heard me preach through the years; others were people who didn't attend the church where I was pastoring. Prior to the first sermon, I gave listeners the list of interview questions I would be using during the interview following the last sermon.

One individual, who had never heard me preach prior to the research sermons, was very methodical in the way he approached life. He took the time to read the questions and proceeded to answer them *before* hearing the first sermon in order to provide a benchmark for himself. He admitted in his first set of answers that while he used to attend church, he hadn't done so in a few years. He felt he was conscious of God in his life, yet he could "do better." Following the four sermons, he answered the questions a second time and acknowledged that significant movement toward the Divine occurred within his heart. During our interview, this man conveyed that these sermons had caused him to "open up to God more." He proceeded to tell me that he didn't typically discuss religious things, but he had told multiple people, including family and coworkers, about these sermons and what they had meant to him. He concluded his conversation with me by saying, "The sermons made me think more about my part in relating to God and helped me grasp that God relates to us on our own level."

Desiring that my research project represent as many cross sections of people as attended my church, I interviewed a few retired people. All of them had grown up in the church and had spent decades listening to sermons. I wondered what they would think of this imaginative, character-developing storytelling style. Did they simply endure my preaching because they were deeply committed to attending church? One of them shared with me that through the years, he had "dreaded" the time in the service when the message was given. He simply wasn't a "sermon person" and had developed a habit of sleeping during the message. However, he said he had paid attention to the sermons with characters from Scripture who were brought to life. Another older participant told me that previous pastors had "taught *about* the Bible, but it wasn't really real." Both of these participants shared that listening to these sermons had been a meaningful experience. They also remarked that their connection to God and their faith had been positively impacted, affecting their everyday lives.

As I was interviewing one individual about the four sermons I had preached for my research, she commented that the series had been meaningful for her, but . . . then she paused. I wondered what she would say next. She continued, "I remember a series of sermons you did a few years ago during Advent. I can still tell you which characters you preached about. I will never forget those sermons. I still think about them. Those sermons have changed the way I think about how God is personally present in my life . . .

especially during Christmas." Identifying with the characters of Luke 1 and 2 impacted her connection with the Divine.

Some of the older congregation members had heard and read the biblical narratives for years. The stories, at times, appeared to be simple children's tales. However, when cultural and historical details were interwoven within sagas of the sacred texts, the experiences of the characters became pertinent to the listeners' lives. Michael Rogness, a former homiletics professor at Luther Seminary and parish preacher, states in his book *Preaching to a TV Generation*, "When the story is retold well, people catch glimpses of things they never heard before, even in the most familiar stories. Old stories become new again. Unexpected insights flood the mind."[2] One particular participant, who had attended church for decades, shared that her experience with these sermons had provided her with intriguing details to ponder and that her mind would wander back to these stories during the week. Even the oldest of saints can experience Scripture afresh and find the accounts life-giving and meaningful.

A Connection with the Divine

I preached the sermons for my original research during Lent. I was devising my plan and having it approved months prior to implementing the project. I was focused on the sermons, the methodology of collecting the necessary data, the structure of the research, and all the requirements for a successful project. I chose the timing of the research based on the availability of participants and the amount of time needed to write a dissertation. To my dismay, I had overlooked the detail of Lent.

To complicate the situation, I had narrowed the scope of my research to only include sermons/texts from the Gospel of John.

In addition, I wanted to honor male and female characters in my development of these sermons. Trying to find a female voice within the Gospel of John proved to be a bit challenging. Months before doing my doctorate, I had preached a couple of sermons on the woman at the well from John 4. I didn't think it would be wise to have my congregation members listen to yet another sermon on that text so soon. The story of Lazarus with his sisters, Mary and Martha, in John 11 appeared to be too lengthy, with multiple layers that would likely be better served in a series, not as a stand-alone sermon. Hence I chose Mary Magdalene in the resurrection narrative (John 20:11–18) as the female representative for the research sermons.

As I began studying and researching for the Mary Magdalene sermon, I was confounded about how to embrace her role in the resurrection story while Lent was still in full swing. I envisioned her as a tenacious and determined person, focused on truth and helping others even while she feared being harmed. (Following the method described in chapter 4, I utilized the DiSC assessment and the Enneagram to shape these particular traits.) This personality profile seemed fitting, since she remained at the cross when many others abandoned Jesus. With those pieces in place, I trudged through sermon preparations and the documentation necessary to include in the research. In my heart and mind, I struggled to release Lent long enough to preach a resurrection sermon.

The Sunday arrived for me to tell the Mary Magdalene story. One of the research participants, "Kathy," invited her friend "Laura" to join her and introduced her to me as the last notes of the musical prelude were being played on the organ. I smiled, said it was nice to meet her, and waved as I headed to the platform for the beginning of the service. At the appropriate time in the service, I stepped to the pulpit to preach the sermon. I told the imaginative story of Mary Magdalene—her feeling helpless instead of helpful, her determination to get things done being thwarted, her grief and dismay at an empty tomb. Acknowledging her thoughts and feelings set the stage for the powerful and gentle words of Jesus when he calls Mary by name as she weeps in the garden. After commenting about the Divine Creator calling Adam by name in the garden of Eden and linking that story to the garden and Jesus calling Mary by name, I moved to the truth that the Divine always calls us by name. I continued by mentioning how loss and grief intrude into our lives. Then as I neared the conclusion of the sermon, I said these words: "The author of John conveyed to the first-century Christ followers and to us that God knows your name. When grief overwhelms us, God lovingly whispers our name, knowing our situation and being fully present to us at all times. When we don't know which way to turn, God lovingly whispers our name, knowing our situation and being fully present to us at all times. When life is unraveling and our determination shrinks in the shadows, God lovingly whispers our name, knowing our despair and grief and being fully present to us at all times."

The service concluded in the usual way, with a song, a benediction, and hand shaking at the door. Most people had left, but I had not seen Kathy and Laura. I peeked into the sanctuary and saw them sitting together; the sound of sniffles and nose blowing was noticeable. I slowly began walking in their direction, wondering if I was intruding. They turned in my direction. Laura stood and turned to face me, her eyes and nose red from crying. She made her way toward me, with Kathy following closely behind her. Pointing over her shoulder, Laura asked, "Did she tell you about me?" Before I could answer, Kathy interjected, "I keep telling her I didn't." The woman I had just met that morning continued talking: "I'm not a religious person at all, and I don't typically go to church. And I don't know how you knew, . . . but a couple of weeks ago, my significant other passed away." Laura fought for composure. I waited for her to continue. "I've been really struggling, . . . and now I know," she said, pointing to the ceiling. "He knows my name."

Unintended Results

My purpose in implementing a preaching style using a biblical imagination focused on the development of the characters was to create space within a sermon that invites the listener to experience the Divine. I cared about the spiritual life of my congregation members, and I longed for them to continue in their journey of being "conformed to the image of his Son" (Rom 8:29). Yet being the preacher, my emphasis was on the preaching event. However, after my parishioners had spent months, maybe years, listening to a variation of this storytelling style with intentional development of the characters, I started to hear a recurring theme in people's comments. Some shared that they were reading their Bibles more than they had in the past because the Scriptures had come alive for them. Some told me they would read a passage and then spend time thinking about it from the character's point of view. They had acquired the ability to move beyond reading Scripture because they knew they "should" or looking for a quick, encouraging word or principle to be learned. They could now wander and wonder with the Spirit about the holy texts. The concept that they could identify with the characters of the Bible impacted their own connection to Scripture.

As preachers, we sometimes need to be encouraged in our attempts to speak a significant word. We can all tell anecdotes about how listeners have connected with the Spirit of God through the preaching event, and we all sometimes wonder what we can say to encourage and challenge the listener. We long to be effective in our sermonizing. While we can agree that it is the work of the Spirit that impacts the hearer, we also know that we play a role in the process sometimes. To keep ourselves and the listener engaged in "hearing the message" (Rom 10:17), we need to try new methods and develop various styles. One participant who was interviewed said, "I wish every minister, every priest, would use this sermon style to varying degrees. It enhances the spiritual understanding and experience." We all, preacher and listener alike, are hungry to know, to connect, to experience the Divine. Frederick Buechner, the renowned author and preacher, challenges us when he states, "The story we are given to tell is a story that smells of [Christ's] life in all its aliveness, and our commission is to tell it in a way that makes it come alive as a story in all its aliveness and to make those who hear it come alive and God knows to make ourselves come alive too."[3] We as preachers desire for our sermons to be meaningful to listeners. Intentionally crafting sermons to allow the characters of Scripture to be fully alive and fully human inclines preacher and listener alike toward a greater openness to the Spirit and a deeper connection to the Divine.

7

Feeding the Soul

I wasn't sure when it happened. I certainly didn't mean for it to happen. Actually, I had been determined that it wouldn't happen. And yet, much to my dismay, Scripture had become a textbook. I knew how to read the text while asking the correct questions: What was the original authorial intent? What theme or themes are being revealed throughout the particular book? Has the English translation appropriately communicated the nuances of the original language in that passage? What might the congregation, those who are listening, need to hear at this specific time? The holy texts, which I used to read as a way of connecting with the Divine, had become literature to study for the purpose of communicating biblical truths to others. Of course, Scripture was important to me; yet it had become much less personal and much more instructive.

As I think back, it seems to me that somehow scholars, professors, and clergy have expected Scripture to be a textbook. When I was pursuing my master of divinity degree, we were taught numerous ways to slice and dice a passage in order to gain an intellectual understanding of the text. We acquired an awareness of the difference between exegesis and eisegesis. We learned about textual criticism, the preservation of ancient manuscripts, and the tedious job of the scribes. We were encouraged to understand the various genres and how a specific style of writing shaped the meaning of a text—whether historical or apocalyptic, the Prophets or the Epistles, poetry or Wisdom. The personal was replaced with the technical. The Psalms, while giving voice to the cry of the heart for many through the centuries, were explained as poetry and songs written in various patterns. Knowledge of the assorted forms could lead to a greater understanding of what the poet was really trying to say. All of these techniques and tools were, and continue to be, valuable.

While my head was gaining knowledge, though, my heart was yearning for my former experience of sitting with my Bible on my lap, having a cup of coffee in my hand, musing and ruminating on a verse or phrase, slowly pondering the passage. I wondered if, in my studies, I was somehow being a less-than-good student, or maybe I was missing out on a technique that would be helpful in answering my heart's longing for the ruminating while attending to the rigors of textual study. I summoned the courage and commented to my Old Testament professor that the Scripture reading required for each week was so extensive that I couldn't take the time to listen for personal nurturing or experience a straight-to-the-heart, cherished message from the text. He immediately replied, "Someday when you are pastoring, you will have a funeral or two within the week, . . . and your congregation will still expect you to have a meaningful sermon on Sunday. Telling them you didn't have time to 'listen' won't work." I turned away feeling deflated and defeated. I knew he was right even before I had experienced that situation for myself.

This phenomenon is one of the hazards of pastoral ministry. After all, it is our job to produce a meaningful message. So we study the sacred writings in order to communicate a pertinent word on Sunday. We analyze the texts to lead Bible studies. We ponder Scripture to write articles and blogs to encourage and inform. We perform these tasks week after week, year after year, and somewhere along the way, we lose the awareness that Scripture is a personal, living word for *us*. We, as preachers and shepherds of the congregations we are called to serve, focus on what others need, wondering how we can bring a relevant word to those precious souls. All the while, we deeply need Scripture to permeate *our* lives. Of course, at times the intellectual experience with Scripture feeds our souls, and yet there are times when I long for something deeper and richer as I navigate the holy texts. Maybe you do too. But how do we pull ourselves away from our engrained approach of using these sacred pages as a textbook? One method might be to sit with the text, allowing our imaginations to help us immerse ourselves in the narratives of Jesus. Let's take a closer look at a methodology that can guide our imaginative encounter with Scripture and the reasons for engaging in this spiritual practice.

Imaginative Prayer and Its Benefits

Although my seminary experience focused on intellectual study, it also included classes on spiritual formation. During one of these classes, I was exposed to the concept of imaginative prayer through Scripture, the practice of allowing my imagination to envision a story of Jesus from the Gospels. I utilized this practice many times through the years before I permitted myself to let it directly impact my sermons.

This practice isn't new. Saint Ignatius of Loyola, one of the founders of the Jesuit order, is credited with utilizing this method in the 1500s. People who were longing for a deeper connection to the Divine would attend retreats where Saint Ignatius directed and guided them in meditation. He instructed them to imaginatively visualize stories of Jesus, to "place [themselves] fully within a story from the Gospels."[1] Ignatius's objective was to empower people to proceed from merely thinking about Jesus to experiencing Christ. Five hundred years after Ignatius's ministry, we still need help in allowing Christ to be more than a theological construct. Often, as clergy, we thrill to think deeply about the Divine and our faith traditions. We thrive as theological thinkers. And yet as humans, we possess joys and sorrows, desires and disappointments, successes and failures. Our holistic nature includes our minds, bodies, and emotions. Consequently, we long for a holistic connection to the Divine. The imaginative meditation that Saint Ignatius taught continues to be a valuable means of relating to Christ in a way that feeds all aspects of our humanness. Ignatius focused on ways to observe and be present within the story.

I suggest we take his approach one step further and shift from solely observing the happenings and characters of the narrative to emotionally identifying with the characters within the blessed narratives. The heart connection with the biblical witnesses is one way of experiencing an emotional connection with Christ, meeting our psychological needs in Christ, just as those who experienced emotional healing when they encountered Jesus. Allowing Scripture to permeate our lives will impact our emotional quests as well. In his book *Prayer: Finding the Heart's*

True Home, Richard Foster writes, "Using the imagination also brings the emotions into the equation, so that we come to God with both mind and heart. It is vitally important to understand the scripture intellectually, but if we have not felt it emotionally, we have not fully understood it."[2] Spiritual maturity changes every aspect of our being, not simply our intellect. After all, we are fully loved by the Lover of our Souls.

When I consider stories in the Gospels, I find that heart transformation and deep relationship occur when humans meet face-to-face with Jesus. The author of the Gospel of John declares his purpose: "But these are written that you may believe that Jesus is the Messiah, the Son of God, and that by believing you may have life in his name" (John 20:31). Transformation, people coming to embrace abundant Divine life, to abide and remain with the Life Giver, saturates the Gospel of John. The woman at the well (chapter 4) is transformed by her encounter with Jesus. The man who once was blind (chapter 9) makes extreme adjustments in his life after meeting Jesus. Lazarus's sister Mary is so transformed—from weeping to rejoicing, from fearing death to embracing resurrection, from limited understanding to greater devotion—as a result of encounters with Jesus that she anoints Jesus at great personal cost (chapter 12).[3] As we imaginatively participate in these tales, our imaginations allow us not just to see but to encounter Jesus, praying all the while that these connections with the Divine transform our hearts and lives. David Benner, psychologist, spiritual director, and retreat leader, states, "God's intention is that we know Divine love by experiencing it."[4] He advocates for using the imagination for meditation guided by the Spirit as a means to deepen our relational knowing of God.

Worries

Some people will have concerns about utilizing our imaginations as a resource for connecting with the Divine, and I would be remiss if I failed to address these concerns. We've been taught to mistrust our imaginations. In this scientific age, we trust facts, but we are suspicious of creative explorations of the mind. Through the years, some preachers have rightfully warned us to be cautious because we are broken and finite as human beings. Scripture itself warns against relying only on our own understanding (Prov 3:5), and yet we have been promised that the Spirit of God will guide us (John 14:16–17; 16:13). Our theology embraces what Scripture teaches—that the Divine has redeemed us, that there is no aspect of our person that is beyond the reach of the Restorer (Rom 8:1–2; Eph 1:7; Col 1:13–14). Certainly, this healing includes our imaginations, especially when we prayerfully ask the Redeemer to guide us.

Distrust in our human imagination is not the only concern we face. At times we hesitate to immerse ourselves in the Scriptures. We hold the texts at arm's length and study them as we would any other inanimate object that can be dissected. This feels safer to us because we recognize the power of the Word, and we know the otherness of Logos. Could it be that we want deeper understanding, more interaction, fuller heart-knowing of the Divine, yet we feel afraid to pursue such riches because we know we can't control this overwhelming, all-encompassing One? We behave like the people of Israel and stand "at a distance" from this Powerful Force (Exod 20:18–21). We recognize we are lacking in wisdom, love, forgiveness, peace, grace, joy, and mercy, yet we are fearful of how we might be changed and to what we might be called if we spend time meeting the One who Sees.

These two worries would be enough to hamper our whole-hearted involvement in imaginative reflection, and yet there's more. In a society that values success and shudders at the thought of failure, we wonder, What if *we* can't create a divine connection in our imaginations? What if *nothing* within our experience resembles the Sacred Other? What does that mean about *us*? What if we cannot access the Divine? When we encounter those fears, we need to remember that God is the Great Initiator. We come to Scripture with expectancy, we receive the Word trusting that there is a word for us, and we acknowledge that the Spirit speaks, guides, and teaches. We wait and listen. Whether we are novices or well practiced at entering into the saga of Scripture through our imaginations, we lean on the Creative One who invites us to a life-giving connection with the Divine. We trust the Trustworthy One to guide us and meet us. We experience a deepening of our relationship by encountering the Holy Other, and at times we experience Divine Silence. When we are confronted with silence, we loosely hold our hope for an interaction with the Spirit, relinquishing our anticipation, and we carry on, returning another time to be with the Lover of our Souls. Please notice I say "when," not "if," we experience silence. Saints through the ages attest to the great silence of the Almighty. We mustn't disregard this reality. After all, the Great Initiator deepens our faith in times of silence as well as times of momentous interaction.

Ways

You may have participated in lectio divina in the past. But in case you are new to the practice, I'll outline the form. Lectio divina is a method of hearing from the Holy Other by way of listening (or reading) a passage and paying attention to what stands out to you. Lectio, as it is often called, isn't about looking for or meditating on the overarching meaning or the exegetical truth of the passage. It is a way of giving space to the Spirit to allow the Divine to speak to our hearts.

Usually, the passage chosen for lectio is only a few verses in length. Longer passages can distract the listener by providing multiple words and phrases. The chosen text is read slowly two or three times, and the listener is encouraged to notice a word or phrase that "sparkles" or "shimmers" or "stands out." The listener prayerfully focuses on that word or phrase and asks the Spirit to guide their thinking to reveal what the Spirit wants the listener to ponder. Multiple variations of the practice have been used through the centuries.

What I am suggesting with the imaginative reflection on a narrative is similar to lectio in that we read the passage two or three times and listen quietly with the Divine. However, when we consider working with a story from Scripture, the passage is likely to be longer than one chosen for lectio. To guide you through the imaginative reflection process, I recommend following the guide on pages 110–11.

Let's look at the text of John 6:25–69. The author of John invites the listener/reader of the text to contemplate who Jesus is. The chapter begins with the story of Jesus feeding the five thousand, an event that would also be meaningful to explore. However, I have chosen the narrative that occurs several verses after that story. After feeding the crowd, the disciples, and eventually Jesus, go to the other side of the Sea of Galilee. The next morning, the crowd goes to Capernaum looking for Jesus.

Within the text, three groups play roles: the crowd (likely not convinced that Jesus is the Messiah), the disciples (those who follow him and have positive leanings toward his messiahship), and the Twelve (also known as the apostles). The passage tells us that the crowd wants Jesus to feed them again, yet Jesus refuses and dives headlong into a teaching, revealing that he is the Bread of Life (v. 35) and has come from the Father (v. 38). The crowd is disappointed, disturbed, and disgusted (vv. 41–42), and the large group of disciples (not the Twelve) "turned back and no longer followed him" (v. 66). Jesus then turns to the Twelve and asks them if they too will leave, and Peter answers, "Lord, to whom shall we go? You have the words of eternal life" (v. 68).

I chose this account because, especially with this text, we preachers and theologians often ponder Jesus's words, debating their meaning and implications while remaining fully locked within our intellect. Yet as we imaginatively immerse ourselves in the narrative, we might experience the passage in a different way. Utilizing our senses will plunge us into the saga.

Here the reflection guide is helpful. What are you hearing, seeing, tasting, smelling? What sensations are you experiencing in your body? With which of the characters do you identify? Are you part of the crowd that feels disappointed that Jesus won't provide as they expect? Are you confused and frustrated? Are you one of the larger groups of disciples? What emotions do you feel when you hear the crowd "grumbl[ing] about him" and "argu[ing] sharply among themselves" (vv. 41, 52)? What is your experience with a teaching that seems so controversial? Or are you one of the insiders, the Twelve? What thoughts and emotions surfaced when other disciples "turned back and no longer followed him" (v. 66)? When Peter makes his declaration (v. 68), how do you respond?

Staying with this narrative of Jesus's teaching, we likely identify with different characters at different times in our lives.

A Guide to Imaginative Reflection

1. **Find a quiet, comfortable setting** that is interruption-free.

2. Take a few moments to **quiet your body, mind, and heart**. Sit comfortably, closing your eyes and taking several deep breaths, focusing on your inhale and exhale.

3. **Whisper a prayer** for the Divine Guide to lead you and to bring to your heart and soul what you need to experience.

4. **Read through the story** slowly a couple of times, and begin to see the story in your imagination. You might approach it as an observer or from the perspective of one of the characters.

5. As you start to visualize the story, **let your senses guide you**. By using them, you no longer merely hear the story; you cross the threshold *into* the story as you ask about and imagine the nuances grasped through your bodily sensations.

    a. What do you **hear**? Go beyond the words of the narrative. Are children playing nearby? Are birds singing or goats bleating?

b. What do you **see**? Look around the setting within your imagination. Are animals parading by? Are merchants hawking wares? Who else is present?

c. Do you **taste** something? Is there a flavor on your lips? Are you anticipating something you will taste soon?

d. What **smells** waft through the air? Are the smells subtle or pungent? Pleasant or obnoxious?

e. What are the **sensations** on your skin? Do you feel the heat from the sun? The coolness of the shade? A gentle breeze? How about your body? Are your muscles stiff from sitting too long? Or sore from being overworked?

6. Expand your experience beyond your senses to **include your emotions.**

a. If **fear** surfaces, what causes that emotion?

b. If **joy** bursts within you, what triggered that reaction?

c. Is there a sudden **frustration** at someone or something?

d. Does **gratitude** overtake you?

7. **Offer a prayer** of thanksgiving for what you experienced.

Sometimes we are like the crowd, annoyed or frustrated that Christ doesn't provide in a way we are hoping or expecting. Or like the larger group of disciples, we encounter a teaching that seems impossible to grasp or participate in, and we contemplate walking away. (An example of a difficult teaching is Christ's teaching of forgiveness. It can be a tough pill to swallow when we have been injured by another's willful action.) Divine Love holds us throughout the entire imaginative process, revealing parts of our hearts that we may not have wanted to see. And yet when we recognize these emotional responses and revelations of our hearts, we can then invite the Healer into our wounds. At some point in our spiritual journey, we might respond with the rhetorical question that Peter asks: "Lord, to whom shall we go?" As we attend to the full happenings and emotions of this narrative by imaginatively experiencing the saga, the passage changes from one for debate and discussion to an incident for heart reflection as we encounter the Bread of Life.

Going Deeper

After participating in an imaginative reflection on Scripture, it is helpful to ponder some questions to guide you as you unpack your experience. Sometimes further understanding comes from analyzing the experience. Here are some questions for you to explore:

* Which character were you, or with whom did you identify within the story?
* What did you notice about the connection between you and that character?
* In the story, what was your experience with Jesus?

✳ In what way does your experience with Jesus in the story impact you?

✳ What might the Divine want you to know?

As we identify areas where the Holy One is speaking truth into our lives, we are encouraged to agree with what the Spirit has shown us.

Viewing biblical characters as wholly dimensioned human beings—with personality styles, archetypal needs, and classic emotions—Allows us to connect with them in the story and, in turn, with the Divine. My hope is that this book will increase the possibility of our identifying with characters within the Holy Narrative. Participating with Scripture in an unfamiliar manner may cause us some consternation at the onset. However, grace abounds! We needn't focus on our success with our experience. We continue to try, knowing the Divine Initiator continues to invite us into God's story.[5]

APPENDIX
Sample Sermon

I want to show you a sermon crafted in the storytelling style proposed in this book. I preached the following sermon at a conference. Due to the nature of the conference, I had time to tackle a longer passage (John 9:1–38) than I typically use for a Sunday service. While the sermon below deals with a larger text, the pattern follows the common flow of my sermons: an opening paragraph or two identifying the point of the sermon to help the listener follow my thought pattern, comments regarding the various contexts of the passage, the imaginative story, and a summary that emphasizes my point. Through the years, I've learned that this progression is a successful method for empowering the listener to come along on the sermon journey.

"Found"

My husband grew up watching *Rudolph the Red-Nosed Reindeer*. It was a Christmas tradition in his home. And still, at some point every Christmas season, we watch the beloved film. In the story, Rudolph doesn't fit in because he has a red nose. He tries to hide it, but it pops out, embarrassing Rudolph and his dad. If the audience somehow misses the theme of fitting in and belonging, the story also has an elf who wants to be a dentist, not a toy maker, and an island of misfit toys. The sense of belonging is significant for human beings.

I marvel at the ways people ostracize other people. I don't like it. When the excluding happens with younger people, I know that they are in a developmental stage when they value being on the "inside" as they find their way in the world. I want to extend grace to them. Yet those of us who are adults know that the tendency to include and exclude others continues far beyond middle school, high school, or even college.

Our society is saturated with "isms" that reveal how much pain we all experience associated with "not belonging." Racism, sexism, classism, ageism . . . the list continues, each one carrying significant pain. In the current political climate, a difference of opinion can rob a person of belonging. We have all experienced the pain of "not belonging." I think the text for today has a message for us.

Every story within Scripture has a context. The verses are found in a specific book from our Christian Scriptures. Every story is located within a historical time and a cultural context. I will do my best to stay true to all of these as I tell the following story. I invite you to use your imagination and join me as we step into a story from Scripture.

(Pause . . . deep breath)

The day began like most days. He awoke in the dark, dressed in the dark, and walked carefully to where he would eat his breakfast.

His mother clicked her tongue, like all mothers do, and smoothed his clothes. There was no reason to not look present-able. He appreciated the care even though it wouldn't matter.

Within a few hours, he would be filthy, the dust of the road sticking to his skin and his garments. That was just the way it was for those who begged along the roadside. He ate his breakfast and was grateful for a good meal. It would be a long day before he had a solid meal again.

He walked along the road, tapping his stick in front of him, carefully taking each step. He wanted to find the right spot for begging. There were several things to consider in choosing a spot. He wanted to be on a road that led to the temple because the foot traffic would be heavier today. But he needed to be far enough away from the other beggars. Beggars were territorial. Sharing might mean less for each one. He understood, but he hated the long hours of . . . hmm, he tried to find the right word—*isolation*. That was it. Sitting all those hours by oneself. A sense of loneliness washed over him.

Being blind already made him different, different from all those who could see, and being different often leads to being left out. He took a deep breath and forcefully exhaled. In his culture, this was certainly true. His society kept "those people" on the outside, the margins. Why, even his faith tradition didn't permit his kind to enter the temple.

He arranged his mat in the perfect place and set his large open box in front of him, hoping he wouldn't miss any of the coins people might toss in his direction. He chuckled to himself. Just listen to him being so deep in thought this early in the day. He shook his head to remove the web of depression and loneliness that was developing.

He liked mornings best. They were less chaotic than afternoons, and the sun wasn't as hot. But the downside to mornings was that fewer people passed by, which meant fewer coins would be dropped in his box.

He heard a family approaching. Oh, how he would have loved to have a family someday. There were adult voices and lots of youthful chatter. He sighed, again. How could he ever have a family when he couldn't even support himself?

Some beggars would call out, trying to get people's attention and get more coins. But he hated calling out. He didn't need to be the center of attention, but being invisible was something completely different. He could tell if those who passed by used this road often. They ignored the beggars and kept right on talking as if the beggars didn't exist. But those who didn't use this road often, well, they typically got really quiet when they passed by. He felt so conflicted. He hated being invisible, but he knew those who did see him felt uncomfortable from his very presence.

He heard another group approaching. Lots of voices. And as they neared, he heard this question: "Rabbi, who sinned, this man or his parents, that he was born blind?"

The blind man cringed. He wanted to shout, "I can hear you! I'm blind, not deaf!" but he bit his tongue. He was accustomed to people acting as though he weren't there.

He shook his head ever so slightly. Sometimes people were so cruel. His parents were good people, yet they had been judged harshly . . . as if, as if having a child born blind were a punishment from God due to some sin they had committed. "What sin? What sin? What sin?" What sin could he have done before he was born? He hated how people gossiped. They could be so cruel.

He didn't know if he even wanted to hear the rabbi's answer. But still he leaned in just a bit to listen, and the rabbi said, "Neither this man nor his parents have sinned. This has happened to reveal the work of God."

What? The blind man had never heard a response like that. No judgment? No shame? The rabbi thought he was important, that he had value. He wasn't just a blind beggar. His life had a purpose. He would reveal the work of God!

Then someone touched him. He started to pull back but then realized that this touch was different. So he paused. Was the hand on his shoulder the rabbi's? Was that who was putting mud on his eyes?

Then the rabbi said, "Go, wash in the Pool of Siloam."

Well, he had to get that mud off his eyes somehow. Besides, there was something within him that compelled him to act on the instructions.

So he did. He went to the pool and washed his eyes. And when he opened them, he could see!

He squinted and blinked many times, trying to get his vision to come into focus. And wow, the sky was bright. No wonder the sun was so warm.

By using the senses that he had relied on all those years, he began to understand what he was seeing. And he headed home.

The neighbors were shocked to see him, and they asked each other, "Is this the man who was born blind?"

With great excitement, he said, "It's me! I can see!"

He started to get even more excited. Could it be? Would he be able to have friends? Would he no longer be an outcast? Could he actually go to the temple and join in the temple festivals?

Neighbors asked him, "How did this happen? What happened that you can see?"

So he told them his story: "A man named Jesus put mud on my eyes and told me to wash in the Pool of Siloam, and I did. And now I can see!"

"Hmmm. Really?" They weren't convinced. "Where's this man now?"

"I don't know."

The neighbors weren't satisfied with the answer the man gave them, so they took him to the religious authorities and told them what they had witnessed. The religious authorities started asking the man questions, and he told them the same story: "A man named Jesus put mud on my eyes and told me to wash in the Pool of Siloam, and I did. And now I can see!"

They kept asking him what happened, and he kept giving the same answer. Then they asked, "Who do you think this man is?"

The man said, "Hmm. I think he's a prophet."

This answer didn't sit well with the religious authorities, and they insisted that the parents of the man who used to be blind be called in. This situation was getting out of hand.

His parents came in for questioning, and they answered the best they could. "Yes," this was their son. "Yes," he had been born blind. The fear that sat in their bellies was making its way toward their throats. They swallowed hard. They knew the authorities had said if someone claimed Jesus was the Messiah, that Jesus came from God, they would be kicked out of the temple. So when asked about their son being able to see, they said that he was of age and could answer the religious leaders' questions himself.

The man who used to be blind felt as though he had been hit in the gut . . . or was it stabbed in the back? But he couldn't blame his parents for trying to stay out of the fray. They had been through enough, with the gossiping and people's insistence that there was "some sin. . . . There's some sin." Being excommunicated would be too much.

And that was when he realized that all his hopes of fitting in, of belonging, of being on the inside, of no longer being an outcast . . . well, those things probably weren't going to happen.

The religious leaders kept asking him questions, and he kept giving them the same answers. One thing led to another, and the religious leaders began hurling insults and accusations at him. Finally, the religious leaders told him, "Get up and get out! And don't come back."

So he did as they said, and he left. As he walked away, he decided to turn off onto a side street where it was quieter. He closed his eyes to shut out the world and retreat into a familiar darkness. He didn't know which was worse . . . to be invisible and ignored or to be rejected and scorned.

Then he heard a familiar voice: "I've been looking for you."

The man opened his eyes, and for the first time, he looked into the face of Jesus.

Jesus continued, "I heard they kicked you out."

The man nodded.

Jesus continued, "Do you want to come with me? Do you want to be one of my followers, one of my friends? You're more than welcome."

The man closed his eyes again. This time he wasn't trying to hide. No, he just wanted to keep the tears from flowing down his face. This man was offering him a friendship, a group to belong to, a chance to no longer be isolated.

Then he opened his eyes. He looked into the face of Jesus, and he knew that Jesus was from God. And he said yes.

(Pause)

We've all had experiences when we know we don't fit in. We've known what it's like to be on the outside, to be in the dark, to feel alone.

There's an important phrase at the end of this chapter. John 9:35 says, "Jesus heard that they had thrown him out, and when he found him . . ." *And when he found him*—Jesus went looking for him, and he looked until he found him. Oh, dear one, no matter what is causing you to feel rejection or isolation or a lack of belonging or a sense of being invisible, listen to the verse again. "Jesus heard that they had thrown him out, and when he found him . . ." The message is clear. Jesus seeks us too. And Jesus finds us too. We are not outside of the Divine Love. We belong; we are included in Christ. Regardless of which "ism" classifies you, regardless of your political bent, regardless of your experience of isolation or rejection, Christ has already found you. God knows. God cares. And God offers us belonging. May we say yes! Amen.

NOTES

Chapter 1

1 Henri Nouwen, *Reaching Out: The Three Movements of the Spiritual Life* (New York: Image Books, 1975), 71.

2 Karl Barth, *Homiletics* (Louisville, KY: Westminster John Knox, 1991), 89.

3 Barth, 80.

Chapter 2

1 Elisabeth R. Jones, "(Re)Discovering a Midrashic Biblical Imagination for the Progressive-Liberal Christian Community" (DMin thesis, Luther Seminary, 2018), 35.

2 Jones, 33–40.

3 Mark Ellingsen, *The Integrity of Biblical Narrative: Story in Theology and Proclamation* (Minneapolis: Fortress, 1990), 47.

Chapter 5

1 Paul Scott Wilson, *The Four Pages of the Sermon: A Guide to Biblical Preaching* (Nashville: Abingdon, 1999), 10–11.

Chapter 6

1 Charles Denison, *The Artist's Way of Preaching* (Louisville, KY: Westminster John Knox, 2006), 60.

2 Michael Rogness, *Preaching to a TV Generation* (Lima, OH: CSS, 1994), 83.

3 Frederick Buechner, *Secrets in the Dark: A Life in Sermons* (New York: HarperCollins, 2006), 86.

Chapter 7

1 David L. Fleming, SJ, "Pray with Your Imagination," IgnatianSpirituality .com, accessed December 4, 2020, https://tinyurl.com/4uvjsxwb.

2 Richard J. Foster, *Prayer: Finding the Heart's True Home* (New York: HarperCollins, 1992), 147–48.

3 For an extensive look at the characters in the Gospel of John and their movement or progress in their relationship with Jesus Christ, see Cornelis Bennema, *Encountering Jesus: Character Studies in the Gospel of John* (Colorado Springs: Paternoster, 2009).

4 David G. Benner, *The Gift of Being Yourself: The Sacred Call to Self-Discovery* (Downers Grove, IL: InterVarsity, 2004), 35.

5 For another scripted approach to utilize with this style of prayer and meditation, check out Spiritual Formation Program of the Grace Institute, "Ignatian Contemplation: Imaginative Prayer with Scripture," Luther College, accessed December 21, 2020, https://www.luther.edu/grace-institute/assets/Ignatian_Contemplation_ _Imaginative_Prayer.pdf.

Working Preacher BOOKS

Good Preaching
Changes Lives

Working Preacher Books is a partnership between Luther Seminary, WorkingPreacher.org, and Fortress Press.

Books in the Series

Preaching from the Old Testament by Walter Brueggemann

Leading with the Sermon by William H. Willimon

The Gospel People Don't Want to Hear: Preaching Challenging Sermons by Lisa Cressman

A Lay Preacher's Guide: How to Craft a Faithful Sermon by Karoline M. Lewis

Preaching Jeremiah: Announcing God's Restorative Passion by Walter Brueggemann

Preaching the Headlines: Pitfalls and Possibilities by Lisa L. Thompson

Honest to God Preaching: Talking Sin, Suffering, and Violence by Brent A. Strawn

Writing for the Ear, Preaching from the Heart by Donna Giver-Johnston

The Peoples' Sermon: Preaching as a Ministry of the Whole Congregation by Shauna K. Hannan

Real People, Real Faith: Preaching Biblical Characters by Cindy Halvorson